HEROES OF THE BIBLE DEVOTIONAL

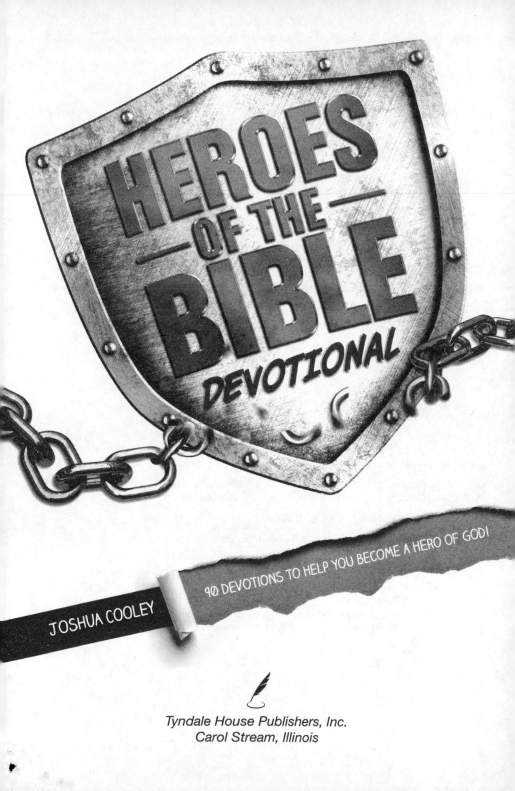

HEROES OF THE BIBLE

DEVOTIONAL

90 DEVOTIONS TO HELP YOU BECOME A HERO OF GOD!

JOSHUA COOLEY

Tyndale House Publishers, Inc.
Carol Stream, Illinois

Visit www.cool2read.com.

TYNDALE and Tyndale's quill logo are registered trademarks of Tyndale House Publishers, Inc.

Heroes of the Bible Devotional: 90 Devotions to Help You Become a Hero of God!

Designed by Nicole Grimes

Edited by Sarah Rubio

For manufacturing information regarding this product, please call 1-800-323-9400.

Library of Congress Cataloging-in-Publication Data

Cooley, Joshua.
  Heroes of the Bible devotional : 90 devotions to help you become a hero of God! / Joshua Cooley.
    pages cm
    ISBN 978-1-4143-8626-3 (sc)
1. Heroes in the Bible—Juvenile literature. 2. Men in the Bible—Juvenile literature. 3. Devotional literature—Juvenile literature. 4. Children—Prayers and devotions. I. Title.
  BS579.H4C67 2014
  220.9′2—dc23
                                   2013040114

Printed in the United States of America

20   19   18   17
7   6   5   4

TO MY FOUR LITTLE PRINCESSES. MAY YOUR
LIVES BE MARKED BY A TOTAL COMMITMENT TO
JESUS, THE GREATEST HERO OF ALL TIME.

CONTENTS

INTRODUCTION

What comes to mind when you hear the word *hero*?

A guy who flies around in a red cape? A superstar athlete who can throw, hit, shoot, or kick a ball better than anyone else? Someone who runs into burning buildings to save lives? A soldier on the front lines fighting for freedom?

Ask 10 different people what a hero is, and you might get 10 different answers. But each definition will almost certainly have to do with human achievement and human glory. That's the way the world works.

The Bible, though, has very different ideas of what a hero is. The list of people who were great in God's eyes might shock you. The Bible's mighty champions didn't wear flashy costumes, possess superpowers, or drive high-powered vehicles. They didn't inspire action figures, bobblehead dolls, or blockbuster summer movies.

Instead, they accomplished amazing things by *God's* power and for *God's* glory. Through faith in their all-powerful Creator, they performed jaw-dropping miracles, conquered mighty armies, and ruled nations. They defeated giants, toppled towering city walls, and raised the dead. They wrote books of the Bible, started churches worldwide, and proclaimed the good news of God's salvation, even in the face of death. These heroes rocked!

Maybe you're thinking, *I'd love to be a hero for God too, but I could never do stuff like that. Those people were way more holy than me.* Not true!

The heroes of the Bible were regular, ordinary people who stubbed their toes, woke up with bed head, and struggled with sin—just like you. They became heroes not because they were superspecial, but because they humbly lived for God. As Matthew 23:11 says, "The greatest among you must be a servant." These incredible men and women achieved greatness by serving God and others.

In this devotional, you'll read about poor heroes, rich heroes, kid heroes, and even a slave hero. You'll learn about bold prophets, powerful kings, and a courageous queen. And you'll see that every single one of them was a normal person, just like you.

Because it's not who you are that matters to God; it's what you allow him to do through you. As the Bible says, by faith you can move mountains (see Matthew 17:20)!

Most important, as you read this book, you'll learn about the greatest hero in history— God's perfect Son, Jesus Christ, who loved you so much that he died for your sins, then rose from the dead so you can live with him forever. Talk about superpowers!

So go ahead . . . turn the page and get started. Through faith and obedience, you can be a true hero for God too!

A TRUE HERO FOR GOD . . . | **BELIEVES THAT GOD CREATED AND RULES EVERYTHING.**

A HERO'S TALE

Let's try an experiment. First, stand up and do a few jumping jacks to limber up. Maybe some sit-ups and push-ups, too. Go ahead. Take your time.

Done? Good. Now, close your eyes, take a deep breath . . . and create an ocean.

Now open your eyes. Did it work? No? Okay, maybe try something smaller, like a mountain. Ready, go!

No mountain either? Hmmm, probably still too big for starters. Better try something even smaller, like a hippo or a walrus. Come back when you're done.

What's that? You couldn't do that either? Well, let's go supersmall. Try creating an acorn or a tadpole or even a gnat. Perhaps you should wave a magic wand and say "Hocus-pocus" or "Abracadabra."

It didn't work, did it? Well, good try anyway. But it's not surprising. After all, you're only human, and humans don't possess the power to create something out of nothing.

But there is someone who can: God.

DECODING THE MESSAGE

Genesis 1:1 says, "In the beginning God created the heavens and the earth." That's the Bible's way of saying that before time or life began, God existed, and he created everything. He created the sun, moon, stars, planets, and galaxies. He created the earth and everything in it—the oceans, rivers, land, mountains, trees, plants, animals, and humans.

He created *everything*!

Remember how you couldn't create even the tiniest creature? Now consider God's incredible power and limitless creative abilities. He created the entire universe simply by speaking. And if he created everything, that means he rules everything too. He can tell his creation what to do because nothing would exist if it weren't for him. He is an indescribably awesome and powerful God!

This is so important to believe. What we believe about the universe's beginning affects everything else in our lives. If you believe that you were created by a random act of nature and not by God, then you'll probably live as if God didn't exist, so you don't have to obey a higher authority. You'll think you can do whatever you want because there are no rules. That's a scary thought.

But if you believe in an all-powerful, all-knowing Creator, that means you *were* created for a reason and you *do* answer to a higher authority. You understand that life isn't all about you. It's about serving the God who created you and learning more about him. It's a wonderful life with meaning and purpose.

And that's no hocus-pocus.

BATTLE PLAN

Memorize what God made on each of the six days of Creation. You can read about it in Genesis 1:1–2:3.

3

A TRUE HERO FOR GOD . . . | **BELIEVES THAT GOD CREATED US TO WORSHIP HIM.**

A HERO'S TALE

Yesterday's devotional talked about God creating everything, including you. But have you ever wondered *why* God created you? In other words, what's your purpose in life?

Lots of people have wrong ideas about this. Some people think life is one big party. Their purpose in life is nothing more than enjoying themselves. Other people live for money and material stuff. Others think they're supposed to work, work, work—from sunrise to sunset every day. Still others think their main purpose is to be as good as possible—go to church, show kindness to others, etc.

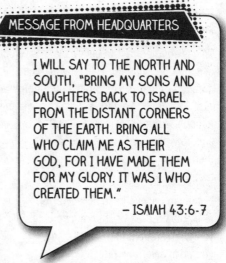

MESSAGE FROM HEADQUARTERS

I WILL SAY TO THE NORTH AND SOUTH, "BRING MY SONS AND DAUGHTERS BACK TO ISRAEL FROM THE DISTANT CORNERS OF THE EARTH. BRING ALL WHO CLAIM ME AS THEIR GOD, FOR I HAVE MADE THEM FOR MY GLORY. IT WAS I WHO CREATED THEM."

– ISAIAH 43:6-7

These things are all good, to a degree. It's important to have fun, to work, to earn money, and to do good deeds. But none of those things, by themselves, are truly why you are here.

The answer is so simple it might surprise you: God created you to worship him.

DECODING THE MESSAGE

As simple as that truth sounds, it's also pretty deep. When we truly understand our purpose in life, it will answer a lot of questions and affect everything we do. It will shift our focus from our selfish desires and put it where it's supposed to be—on God. Life is not about us. It's about God—because we wouldn't be here without him.

Just like a soldier needs to understand the mission in order to be effective in battle, we must understand that we live to worship God. Worship is simply giving God the glory he deserves as the eternal, almighty, all-knowing Creator of the universe.

Many people associate worship with singing praise music to God. That's one form of worship, but certainly not the only one. We should glorify God in *everything* we do, because that's why God made us, as today's verse says. Whatever you're good at—sports, music, math, science, art—you can worship God in it by giving him the glory for your success.

Need more ideas on how to worship God? Obeying your parents is worship toward God. So is praying, reading the Bible, memorizing Scripture, listening in church, helping others, and telling a friend about Jesus.

There are countless ways to worship our Creator. Time to pick some and get started!

BATTLE PLAN

Make a list of three ways you can worship God this week (ask your parents to help, if needed) and do them!

DAY 3

UNDERSTANDS HE IS A SINFUL REBEL WHO NEEDS A SAVIOR.

A HERO'S TALE

Think about the most beautiful places on earth: Maui. Tahiti. The Bahamas. The French Riviera. Now imagine a place a thousand times better, where the natural beauty was surpassed only by the fact that God himself walked there.

> ### MESSAGE FROM HEADQUARTERS
>
> GOD SHOWED HIS GREAT LOVE FOR US BY SENDING CHRIST TO DIE FOR US WHILE WE WERE STILL SINNERS.
> – ROMANS 5:8

That was the Garden of Eden.

Adam and Eve had it made. As the Garden's only residents, humanity's first man and woman lived in a literal paradise on earth—a perfect, sinless home where God personally interacted with them (see Genesis 3:8). What a life!

But Adam and Eve chose to forfeit this amazing experience. When Satan tempted them to disobey God by eating the Garden's forbidden fruit, they decided to rebel against their Creator. They chose their way instead of God's. (You can read about this catastrophe, also known as the Fall, in Genesis 3.)

So sin and death entered the world. Man was separated from God, and God's perfect creation fell into disorder.

DECODING THE MESSAGE

Adam and Eve really blew it. But we can't be too hard on them, because we eventually would've messed up too.

Ever since Adam and Eve's original sin, we've all sinned. Sin is breaking God's laws, and the Bible says that we are all sinners (see Romans 3:23). In fact, we're born into sin (see Psalm 51:5). We've inherited a sinful nature from Adam. From the moment we come into the world, our natural tendency is to shake our fists at our Creator and say, "I don't want to follow your rules. I know best!"

That's not only foolish; it's downright wicked. Being just and holy, God could have chosen to destroy us. He could've thought, *You know what? These people aren't worth my time. I made them and gave them everything they need, and now they're rebelling against me. Time to wipe them out.*

But God didn't do that. Rather than react in angry justice (which he had every right to do), God chose to show us undeserved love and mercy by providing a path of salvation. He did that by sending his perfect Son, Jesus Christ, to die for our sins.

We are all born as sinful rebels who desperately need a Savior. Praise God that he gave us exactly what we needed, not what we deserved!

BATTLE PLAN

Read Ephesians 2:1-10. It's a wonderful passage that shows how much we needed God and what he's done for us through Christ.

ABEL: THE HERO WHOSE WORSHIP PLEASED GOD

A TRUE HERO FOR GOD . . .   OFFERS PROPER SACRIFICES TO GOD.

A HERO'S TALE

After reading that statement above, you might be thinking, *Whoa, hold on. I'm supposed to offer sacrifices—like killing sheep and burning them on an altar?*

Not exactly. We'll explain in a moment. But first, a little background . . .

After Adam and Eve's sin in the Garden of Eden, the world became a very different place. Sin made everything difficult. Still, God lovingly watched over Adam and Eve, and he blessed them with lots of children. Their first two were Cain and Abel. You can read their story in Genesis 4.

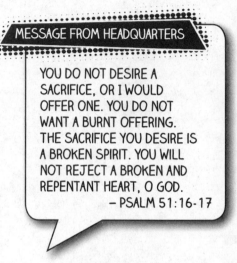

MESSAGE FROM HEADQUARTERS

YOU DO NOT DESIRE A SACRIFICE, OR I WOULD OFFER ONE. YOU DO NOT WANT A BURNT OFFERING. THE SACRIFICE YOU DESIRE IS A BROKEN SPIRIT. YOU WILL NOT REJECT A BROKEN AND REPENTANT HEART, O GOD.
                                    – PSALM 51:16-17

Cain was a farmer, and Abel was a shepherd. One day, both brothers brought sacrifices to God. Cain offered his fruits and vegetables, and Abel gave the best of his flocks.

God was pleased with Abel's sacrifice but not Cain's. Filled with jealousy and rage, Cain killed Abel and then tried to hide his sin. As punishment, God forced Cain to become a wanderer for the rest of his life.

DECODING THE MESSAGE

This tragic story teaches us a lot about worshiping God, even though we don't have to sacrifice animals anymore. Why was God pleased with Abel's sacrifice and not Cain's? It seems that Abel brought his offering with a heart that wanted to please God, while

Cain did not. Abel was a hero because he gave his best to God—"the best portions of the firstborn lambs from his flock" (Genesis 4:4).

Are you giving your best to God? Are you diligently seeking him through his Word and prayer? Do you obey your parents? Do you listen attentively in church? Are you using the gifts and abilities God has given to you (in music, sports, art, academics, etc.) for his glory?

These are sacrifices we can offer to God today. Like our verse says, God wants our hearts more than anything. He doesn't *need* anything from us, as if he were lacking it without us. (As almighty God, he already owns everything!) But by our sacrifices, we can show him a "broken and repentant" (humble) heart that seeks to follow him, as today's verse says. He wants our desires, thoughts, and actions to all be focused on worshiping him.

BATTLE PLAN

List 5 to 10 ways you can give your best to God, and put your list somewhere you'll see it every day.

GOSPEL CONNECTION

Don't throw any sheep on an altar! Because Jesus, the perfect Lamb of God, sacrificed himself on the cross, no more sacrifices for sins are needed. To receive God's forgiveness, we just need to trust in what Jesus has already done.

A TRUE HERO FOR GOD . . .

HUMBLY TURNS FROM HIS SINFUL NATURE THROUGH FAITH.

A HERO'S TALE

Quick pop quiz: Who were history's first babies? If you guessed Cain and Abel, you're correct!

God created Adam as a grown man (from the dust of the ground), and he created Eve as an adult woman (from one of Adam's ribs). But Cain and Abel—and the rest of mankind—came into being through a mother giving birth.

MESSAGE FROM HEADQUARTERS

WHEN ADAM SINNED, SIN ENTERED THE WORLD. ADAM'S SIN BROUGHT DEATH, SO DEATH SPREAD TO EVERYONE, FOR EVERYONE SINNED.
— ROMANS 5:12

Even as babies, Cain and Abel had a sin problem. Because of their parents' disobedience in the Garden of Eden, Cain and Abel inherited a sinful nature. In other words, they were born with hearts that naturally opposed God. This separated them from God, just like their parents had to leave God's presence in the Garden.

Life wasn't easy for Cain and Abel. Suffering, pain, and death—all of which had never been part of God's original creation—were now a reality for them.

But God still loved Cain and Abel. As the brothers grew up, Cain struggled greatly with his sinful nature even though God lovingly warned him, "If you refuse to do what is right, then watch out! Sin is crouching at the door, eager to control you. But you must subdue it and be its master" (Genesis 4:7).

You know the rest of the story. Cain gave in to his evil desires and committed a horrible crime, killing his own brother. He never seemed to truly repent or turn to God in faith.

However, Abel seemed to get it right before his untimely death. He loved God and offered pleasing sacrifices. By God's grace, Abel overcame his sinful nature with a humble heart that wanted to obey God through faith (see Hebrews 11:4).

DECODING THE MESSAGE

Like Cain and Abel, we are all born with a sin problem. Thousands of years have passed since the Garden of Eden, but every human still starts life with a sinful nature. And if our sin is not forgiven, we'll be eternally separated from God. The Bible is very clear about this. But God loved us so much that he offered his own Son, Jesus, on the cross as a sacrifice for sins so that we could be forgiven.

We have a choice. We can choose to be like Cain, who ignored God's warning. Or we can be like Abel, who trusted in God's plan of salvation and turned from his sin.

The choice seems obvious. Which will you choose?

BATTLE PLAN

To learn more about our sinful natures and God's plan of salvation, read Romans 5. If you need help understanding it, ask one of your parents or another trusted adult.

DAY 6

A HERO'S TALE

The story of Cain and Abel is a tragic tale.

Abel had so much promise, so much to live for. Sin was changing the world around him for the worse, but he took a stand for righteousness. Having trusted in his Creator, he chose to follow God rather than live as he pleased. Then, in one swift act of fury, Cain took his brother Abel's life.

> **MESSAGE FROM HEADQUARTERS**
>
> GOD CREATED HUMAN BEINGS IN HIS OWN IMAGE. IN THE IMAGE OF GOD HE CREATED THEM; MALE AND FEMALE HE CREATED THEM.
>
> — GENESIS 1:27

It took only two generations of human existence for the first murder to be committed. That might seem shocking at first. But if you know anything about sin, it's actually not surprising at all. Sin is wickedly deceitful. Anger and unkind thoughts, for instance, can quickly turn into something much worse if left unchecked. Just ask Cain.

Abel's murder was a horrible act in so many ways. But the worst part about it? Cain's terrible deed was an attack on God's image.

DECODING THE MESSAGE

The Bible says all humans are created in God's image. This makes us different from anything else God created. Other mammals, birds, and fish weren't created in God's image. Neither were trees or mountains or planets. Only people.

To be made in God's image means to be like God. That doesn't mean we're identical to God. He is holy, all-knowing, all-powerful, and present everywhere. We are not. But we do share certain characteristics. Like God, we can speak, reason, love, and show creativity. We are spiritual in nature. As God's image bearers, we represent God and are more special to him than anything else he created.

Can you see now why Cain's murder of Abel was so terrible? Abel, like every person, was God's image bearer, and Cain destroyed him.

Knowing that we are made in God's image should affect how we treat others. A true hero for God values all human life because humans are God's representatives. It doesn't matter if you're white, black, brown, or polka-dot! All people are made in God's image, and he loves everyone equally.

If you tease people for the way they look, you are attacking God's image. If you treat someone badly because his or her skin color is different from yours, you are attacking God's image. If you make fun of someone with a disability, you are attacking God's image.

God doesn't make mistakes. He made you just the way he wanted to. Same with everybody else. So value all human life.

BATTLE PLAN

Make friends with someone who is different from you. It's honoring to God, and you'll be surprised by what you can learn.

NOAH

NOAH: THE HERO OF THE GREAT FLOOD

DAY 7

A TRUE HERO FOR GOD . . .   LIVES FOR GOD IN A SINFUL WORLD.

A HERO'S TALE

Things weren't just bad. They were downright awful.

When Adam and Eve disobeyed God in the Garden of Eden, sin didn't quietly tiptoe into the world like a thief sneaking into a house; it charged in like an Old West cattle stampede. Nine generations later, mankind had become so wicked, Genesis 6 describes it this way:

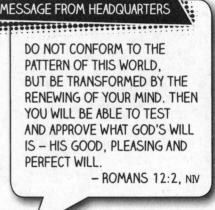

MESSAGE FROM HEADQUARTERS

DO NOT CONFORM TO THE PATTERN OF THIS WORLD, BUT BE TRANSFORMED BY THE RENEWING OF YOUR MIND. THEN YOU WILL BE ABLE TO TEST AND APPROVE WHAT GOD'S WILL IS – HIS GOOD, PLEASING AND PERFECT WILL.
— ROMANS 12:2, NIV

- "Everything [humans] thought or imagined was consistently and totally evil" (v. 5).
- "The Lord was sorry he had ever made [humans] and put them on the earth. It broke his heart" (v. 6).
- "God saw that the earth had become corrupt and was filled with violence" (v. 11).

Humans were failing the test of life. But one man was different. Genesis 6:9 says, "Noah was a righteous man, the only blameless person living on earth at the time, and he walked in close fellowship with God." While everyone else was choosing wrong, Noah chose right. As humanity fell apart all around him, he stood strong for God.

DECODING THE MESSAGE

It's hard to be different. Our natural desire is to fit in with others. Nobody likes to be the oddball.

But if you're a Christian, God calls you to be different from the sinful world around you. Today's verse, Romans 12:2, says, "Do not conform to the pattern of this world, but be transformed by the renewing of your mind" (NIV).

The word *conform* means to fit into a mold. Do you remember playing with Play-Doh? If you press a lump of Play-Doh into a mold, the Play-Doh comes out shaped like the mold.

As humans, we are kind of like Play-Doh. We're very moldable. But God doesn't want the wicked world we live in to shape us. *He* wants to shape us!

The first step in allowing God to shape you is acknowledging your sins and putting your faith in him. You must trust that God knows what's best for you.

Then you need to read the Bible (that's the "renewing of your mind" part of Romans 12:2). Praying and obeying your parents are really important too. And avoid following the crowd when the crowd goes against God's Word. These are all ways to live for God in a sinful world.

Be Play-Doh in God's hands, not the world's!

BATTLE PLAN

Set up a daily Bible reading plan. The more you conform to God's Word, the less you'll conform to the world around you.

DAY 8

A HERO'S TALE

Like a fast-spreading plague, sin had completely infested the earth. Mankind's wickedness and rebellion grieved God. So God told Noah, the only righteous man alive, that he was going to cleanse the earth with a worldwide flood. Then God commanded Noah to build an ark so he and his family would be saved.

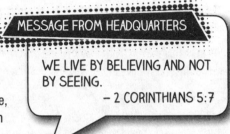

MESSAGE FROM HEADQUARTERS

WE LIVE BY BELIEVING AND NOT BY SEEING.
— 2 CORINTHIANS 5:7

Noah probably wondered, *Flood? Ark? What are those?* After all, the story of Noah is the first time the Bible ever mentions a rainstorm. Noah certainly had never seen a flood or an ark before.

What's more, God was asking Noah to perform an *enormous* construction task, never before done. The ark was longer than a football field and about four stories tall! Noah and his three sons had to build it by themselves, without power tools or machines.

As Noah worked, people passing by must have given him strange looks and maybe even taunted him: "There's that crazy Noah. What on earth is he building?"

Despite all this, "Noah did everything exactly as God had commanded him" (Genesis 6:22). Noah was living by faith, not by sight.

DECODING THE MESSAGE

Human sight is an amazing thing. Our eyes are information collectors. When they see something, they send that information to our brains through the optic nerve. Then our brains process the information, make decisions, and send our bodies into action by telling our nerves and muscles how to respond.

Without sight, it's hard to believe or do things. But God often asks us to believe and obey without seeing. It's called faith (see Hebrews 11:1), and we can't please God without it (see Hebrews 11:6).

When God told Noah about the ark and the flood, Noah couldn't see what God was planning. He had no idea what a flood was or how to build an ark. He just had to believe and obey. This made Noah a hero of faith!

What is God calling you to do by faith and not by sight? Whatever it is, trust God. If he can miraculously save Noah from a worldwide flood, he is worthy of your faith too!

BATTLE PLAN

Read Hebrews 11, which is often called the "Hall of Faith." It's all about biblical heroes, including Noah, who lived by faith and not by sight.

GOSPEL CONNECTION

The greatest way we can live by faith and not by sight today is to believe that Jesus died on the cross for our sins and rose from the dead more than 2,000 years ago. We didn't see it happen, but the Bible says we must believe these truths to be saved.

A TRUE HERO FOR GOD . . . IS GRATEFUL FOR GOD'S MERCY.

A HERO'S TALE

Here's a pop quiz: What is a rainbow?

A. A multicolored arc in the earth's atmosphere that is caused by the reflection of light in water droplets.

B. A sign of God's promise to never destroy the earth again by flood.

C. Something that leprechauns keep their pots of gold at the end of.

D. Answers A and B.

MESSAGE FROM HEADQUARTERS

THE LORD OUR GOD IS MERCIFUL AND FORGIVING, EVEN THOUGH WE HAVE REBELLED AGAINST HIM.
– DANIEL 9:9

If you answered choice D, you're correct! Rainbows are amazing meteorological phenomena that occur when the sun comes back out during or after rainstorms. But rainbows are also a reminder—a thousands-of-years-old reminder—of God's love and mercy.

God showed both to Noah during the Great Flood of Genesis 7–8. When the rain stopped and the floodwaters receded, Noah's ark came to rest on Mount Ararat. Finally, after more than a year inside the ark, Noah and his family stepped on dry ground again. There, Noah worshiped God by offering a sacrifice.

God put a rainbow in the sky and made a promise to Noah: "I will never again curse the ground because of the human race, even though everything they think or imagine is bent toward evil from childhood. I will never again destroy all living things" (Genesis 8:21).

And ever since then, God has stayed true to his word.

DECODING THE MESSAGE

In the story of Noah's ark, Noah's faith is remarkable. So is the God-ordained miracle of everything in the ark surviving the Flood. But the greatest part of the story is the mercy of God.

You see, God would have been completely justified if he had washed away Noah and his family in the Flood, along with everyone else. As great as Noah was, he didn't deserve to be saved. Noah was a sinner just like us, and the Bible is very clear that sin deserves death (see Romans 6:23).

God doesn't owe us anything. Our hearts are naturally rebellious toward him. Whatever good we receive from him is a gift, not a right. We deserve punishment and death. But God gives us mercy anyway (and a lot of rainbows!) because he loves us so deeply.

Noah understood this and worshiped God. That should be our response to God's mercy too!

BATTLE PLAN

Memorize today's Bible verse. It's a great reminder of God's mercy toward us.

GOSPEL CONNECTION

God's greatest act of mercy was sending Jesus to die for us. He could've easily let us die in our sins—that's what we deserved. But in his mercy, God gave us what we *didn't* deserve—a chance for salvation through his perfect Son!

A TRUE HERO FOR GOD . . .   ANSWERS GOD'S CALL.

A HERO'S TALE

Abraham was a man of great faith. Nobody argues that. To trust in God the way he did throughout his life was remarkable. But to understand the magnitude of his story, a little history lesson is needed.

> ## MESSAGE FROM HEADQUARTERS
>
> ABRAM DEPARTED AS THE LORD HAD INSTRUCTED.
> – GENESIS 12:4

Abraham came from Ur, a city in ancient Mesopotamia. As city names go, "Ur" ranks pretty low on the creativity scale. It sounds like the noise you make when you get lima beans for dinner or stub your toe. *Urrrrrr!*

The ancient Mesopotamians worshiped many false gods. Abraham's own family did too (see Joshua 24:2). So when God told Abraham—or Abram, as he was called at the time—to leave his home and travel to Canaan, where God would make him into a "great nation" (see Genesis 12:1-3), Abram probably had a lot of questions:

- Who is this God telling me to leave my home country?
- What about all the other gods my family believes in? Aren't they real too?
- Why do I have to go to Canaan? It's a difficult, 1,000-mile journey that will take several months.
- What if the Canaanites don't want me there? And what if I don't like it?
- To become a great nation, I need children. But how is that possible since my wife, Sarai, has been childless her whole life and is now too old to give birth?

Abram had many reasons to say no to God. But instead, he said yes. Before you could say "stub your toe" in ancient Mesopotamian (nope, no idea how to translate that), he had started his journey.

DECODING THE MESSAGE

In many ways, we're not that different from Abram. You see, God calls each of us to do something too. He probably won't call you to travel 1,000 hot, dusty miles on a camel. But he *will* call you to use your God-given gifts and abilities to serve him somehow. And don't be surprised if God's call isn't what you expected in its timing or purpose. That's often how he works.

You might not know why God is calling you to do it, or even how to make it happen. But that's not the point. Abram could've used those things as excuses, too, but he didn't.

Your most important job is to take the first step in faith. True heroes for God answer his call because they know that the God who calls them to do great things will also strengthen them for the task.

God calls all his children to do something. How will you answer?

BATTLE PLAN

Pray about what God is calling you to do for his glory and ask him for the faith to obey.

A TRUE HERO FOR GOD . . .

BELIEVES GOD CAN DO THE IMPOSSIBLE.

A HERO'S TALE

It was a beautiful, clear night. Countless stars twinkled above like tiny diamonds against black velvet.

Lying inside his tent, Abram was worried. It had been some time since God had promised to make him into a great nation. But Abram still had no son. And now, he was probably in his 80s, and his wife, Sarai, was in her 70s. How could they have a baby at that age?

MESSAGE FROM HEADQUARTERS

I AM THE LORD, THE GOD OF ALL THE PEOPLES OF THE WORLD. IS ANYTHING TOO HARD FOR ME?
– JEREMIAH 32:27

God knew Abram was troubled. So God told him to go outside his tent. "Look up into the sky and count the stars if you can," God told him. "That's how many descendants you will have!" (Genesis 15:5).

It was a bold, seemingly impossible promise. But then something strange happened. Abram stopped worrying and trusted God. As Genesis 15:6 says, "Abram believed the LORD, and the LORD counted him as righteous because of his faith."

That night changed everything for Abraham. The man who once lived among pagan idol worshipers had become a child of the living God. Because of Abraham's faith, God gave his righteousness to Abraham and forgave all his sins (see Romans 4).

DECODING THE MESSAGE

Lots of things in life seem impossible to us:

- breathing underwater without an oxygen tank
- reaching the moon without a spaceship
- finishing the final level of your favorite video game
- enjoying a trip to the dentist

But nothing is impossible for God.

We're talking about the Lord God Almighty here! He created the entire universe simply by speaking. He breathed life into dust and formed mankind. He holds the planets in their orbits. He controls nature and has power over death. He transforms wicked hearts.

Nothing is too difficult for him.

Are you worried about anything? Do you lie awake at night feeling anxious? Do you fret about something out of your control?

Worrying is like saying, "God, I believe you can do lots of things, but this problem is a little too big for you." And that's just not true.

Abraham learned that firsthand. God eventually gave him a son, Isaac. Then Isaac had kids, and grandkids, and great-grandkids, and on and on. Pretty soon, the nation of Israel was born and Abraham's descendants were too many to count, just like God had promised!

Whatever your situation is, trust God. He can do the impossible!

BATTLE PLAN

Ask your parents or other trusted adults who love God to tell you about a time when the Lord did the seemingly impossible for them. The older they are, the more stories they are sure to have!

DAY 12

WAITS PATIENTLY FOR GOD'S TIMING.

A HERO'S TALE

Tick, tock, tick, tock . . .

The hours and days passed slowly. Weeks turned into months. Months turned into years. Years turned into decades. And still, Abram waited for God to keep his word.

> **MESSAGE FROM HEADQUARTERS**
>
> I WAITED PATIENTLY FOR THE LORD TO HELP ME, AND HE TURNED TO ME AND HEARD MY CRY.
>
> – PSALM 40:1

When God promised to make Abram into a great nation, Abram was about 75 years old and his wife, Sarai, was about 65—too old to have a baby under normal circumstances. Yet as we learned in yesterday's devotion, Abram put his faith in God's promise.

But nothing happened immediately. Abram waited . . . and waited . . . and waited. He grew older. His hair became grayer. His strength waned.

Occasionally, doubts crept in—*Is God really going to keep his promise? Has he forgotten about me? Was it all just a dream?*—and God had to reassure Abram. God even gave Abram and Sarai new names—Abraham and Sarah—as a sign confirming his promise. Finally, when Abraham was 100 years old and Sarah was 90, God gave them a child—baby Isaac, the son of the promise.

DECODING THE MESSAGE

Abraham waited a whopping 25 years for God's promise to be fulfilled. That's a long time!

We usually think of heroes as men and women of bold action. And that's often true. But godly heroes also know how to wait patiently on the Lord.

As Abraham learned, God is never slow in keeping his promises, and he never forgets. He is always in control and has a perfect plan for our lives.

But his timing is not like ours. He does things according to his schedule, not ours. And that's a good thing, because he is God and we are not. He is perfect in knowledge and power. He can do whatever he wants, whenever he wants. But he *always* does what's best for us. Isn't that awesome?

God wants us to ask him for things. Scriptures like Psalm 5:3, Matthew 7:7-11, Ephesians 6:18, Philippians 4:6, and James 1:5 make that very clear. But we must be prepared to wait for God's answer and trust that we are in good hands while we wait.

During the waiting period, God teaches us important lessons. Waiting produces perseverance, patience, and trust. It's like a plateful of green beans—you might not like it at the time, but they're very good for you.

Whatever you are waiting for, trust in God. He will do what's best for you in his perfect timing.

BATTLE PLAN

Keep a prayer journal of the things you ask of God. Track when and how he answers to see his faithfulness at work!

DAY 13

AVOIDS PRIDEFUL BOASTING.

A HERO'S TALE

MESSAGE FROM HEADQUARTERS

In Genesis 37, we are introduced to a spoiled 17-year-old boy named Joseph. His father, Jacob (Abraham's grandson), loved him more than any of his 11 brothers. Jacob lavished his love on Joseph and paid special attention to him.

AS THE SCRIPTURES SAY, "IF YOU WANT TO BOAST, BOAST ONLY ABOUT THE LORD."
— 2 CORINTHIANS 10:17

This made Joseph's brothers terribly jealous. They hated Joseph and the special treatment he got from Jacob. To make matters worse, when Joseph was tending Jacob's sheep with four of his older brothers, "Joseph reported to his father some of the bad things his brothers were doing" (Genesis 37:2). Sounds like Joseph might have been a tattletale.

After this, Jacob gave Joseph—and only Joseph—a beautiful, multicolored coat. Joseph's brothers grew more jealous. Then Joseph decided to share a dream he had with his brothers.

"So in this dream," he told them, "we were all in the fields tying up bundles of grain. Suddenly, all of your bundles bowed down to my bundle. Pretty cool, huh?"

You can imagine how well that went over with his brothers. But Joseph didn't stop there. Soon, he told his brothers about a second dream.

"Hey, guys," he said, "you'll never believe this, but I had another crazy dream. This time, Dad and Mom were the sun and moon, and you guys were stars. And all of you were bowing down to me again. Go figure!"

Joseph's brothers were so angry, they threw him in a deep well, sold him to slave traders (who took him to Egypt), and lied to Jacob by telling him that Joseph was dead.

DECODING THE MESSAGE

What Joseph's brothers did was terrible. But Joseph didn't help matters any. Even though God gave him those fascinating dreams, Joseph certainly didn't have to tell his brothers. That was boasting.

Boasting is another word for bragging, or speaking too highly of yourself. And the Bible says that's wrong.

Sadly, today's society promotes pride everywhere, especially among our cultural heroes, like movie stars and professional athletes. Have you ever watched an NFL game? It seems like players show off after every single play.

But true biblical heroes are to act differently. Luke 9:48 says, "Whoever is the least among you is the greatest," and Matthew 20:16 says, "The last will be first, and the first will be last" (NIV). That doesn't leave any room for boasting about yourself.

True heroes for God stay humble and boast only in their Creator. In other words, they give God credit for anything they do well. After all, he's the only reason we can do anything at all!

BATTLE PLAN

Write down 5 to 10 things you do well. Then prayerfully boast in the Lord about them, giving him all the glory!

DAY 14

BELIEVES THAT GOD ALWAYS DOES WHAT'S BEST FOR HIM.

A HERO'S TALE

Early on, Joseph endured terrible difficulties.

When he was 17, his angry, jealous brothers sold him into Egyptian slavery. Over the next 13 years, Joseph endured lies, mistreatment, unjust imprisonment, and abandonment. (Read about it in Genesis 37, 39, and 40.)

Sitting alone in a dark, cold, Egyptian dungeon, Joseph probably often wondered, *Where is God? Why is he letting all this happen to me? Does he still love me?*

MESSAGE FROM HEADQUARTERS

WE KNOW THAT GOD CAUSES EVERYTHING TO WORK TOGETHER FOR THE GOOD OF THOSE WHO LOVE GOD AND ARE CALLED ACCORDING TO HIS PURPOSE FOR THEM.
— ROMANS 8:28

Then, suddenly, things got better. Joseph interpreted Pharaoh's dreams about a coming famine and earned a one-way ticket into the royal palace. By age 30, Joseph was Pharaoh's second-in-command. Shortly thereafter, he almost single-handedly saved Egypt (and many other countries) from starvation during a terrible worldwide famine.

As the food shortage spread, even his brothers traveled to Egypt looking for food. They bowed before Joseph, not realizing it was Joseph. His earlier dreams about his family had come true!

When Joseph revealed his identity to his brothers, they were frightened. They thought he might take revenge for their cruelty years earlier. But Joseph saw the big picture: "You intended to harm me, but God intended it all for good. He brought me to this position so I could save the lives of many people" (Genesis 50:20).

DECODING THE MESSAGE

As the years passed, Joseph began to understand God's master plan for his life.

God knew all along that a terrible famine was coming, so to save Jacob's family (which would later become the 12 tribes of Israel), God allowed Joseph to be enslaved, shipped to Egypt, and imprisoned—all to exalt Joseph at the proper time. In essence, God used the wicked deeds of Joseph's brothers to send Joseph ahead of them into Egypt and save them years later. Incredible!

God still works the same way today. Sometimes in our lives, it seems like everything is going wrong and God doesn't care. But nothing could be further from the truth.

God does care (more than you know!), and he works everything out for the good of those who love him. Read today's verse, Romans 8:28, and let that truth sink into your heart.

God will take everything bad that happens to his children and ultimately use it for good. Not just *some* things . . . *everything*!

God *always* has our best in mind. What an amazing God!

BATTLE PLAN

Are you currently going through a trial? Pray about it, track it in a journal, and watch how God turns it into good. Write down the ending, too, so you can remember God's faithfulness. And if your trial doesn't end quickly, don't worry—God still loves you and is working in the situation. Look for ways God is doing good things in the midst of the difficulty.

GOSPEL CONNECTION

Still not convinced God always does what's best for you? Consider this: he lovingly sent his own Son, Jesus Christ, who had no sin, to die for *your* sins. If God was willing to do that, he certainly has your best in mind at all times!

DAY 15

REPAYS EVIL WITH GOOD.

A HERO'S TALE

Joseph's brothers were quivering in their robes.

They couldn't believe their ears. The powerful Egyptian ruler standing before them had just claimed to be Joseph, their long-lost brother whom they had sold into slavery more than 20 years before. It couldn't really be him . . . could it? *Gulp!*

MESSAGE FROM HEADQUARTERS

LOVE YOUR ENEMIES! DO GOOD TO THOSE WHO HATE YOU. BLESS THOSE WHO CURSE YOU. PRAY FOR THOSE WHO HURT YOU.

— LUKE 6:27-28

Earlier, when Joseph's brothers had arrived in Egypt to buy food, Joseph recognized them, but they didn't recognize him. The brothers had bought food from Joseph and dined with him without realizing who he was. (Joseph undoubtedly looked much different after living in Egypt for so long.)

Finally, Joseph couldn't control his emotions anymore. On one of his brothers' visits to Egypt, he blurted out, "It's me, Joseph—your brother!"

His brothers were stunned. But amazement and disbelief quickly turned into fear. As Genesis 45:3 says, "His brothers were not able to answer him, because they were terrified at his presence" (NIV).

They remembered how cruel they had once been to Joseph. Filled with anger and jealousy, they had plotted to kill him before throwing him in a pit and selling him into slavery for a measly 20 pieces of silver.

Now, all these years later, Joseph, as Pharaoh's second-in-command, possessed the power to destroy his brothers. But he didn't. Instead, he threw his arms around them, wept tears of joy, and invited them to live with him in Egypt.

Despite his brothers' wickedness against him, Joseph forgave them. He repaid evil with good.

DECODING THE MESSAGE

Have you ever said any of the following?

- "He hit me first."
- "She deserved it."
- "I'll show him."
- "Someone had to teach him a lesson."

It's easy to justify revenge, isn't it? If someone wrongs us, our natural reaction is to want to pay him or her back. But that attitude is always motivated by sin. Retaliation never pleases God.

He wants us to act differently. We are to show love and respect to others, no matter how difficult it is. That's what Jesus taught us (see today's verse).

God wants his children to repay evil with good. After all, that's what he did for us. We are all wicked sinners who have continually rebelled against God. But rather than repay our evil with the punishment we deserve, God sent his Son, Jesus, to die for our sins. That's amazing love . . . and a great example to follow!

BATTLE PLAN

Seek out someone who has mistreated you and do something kind to him or her. Not only will you please God, but you'll also shock that person!

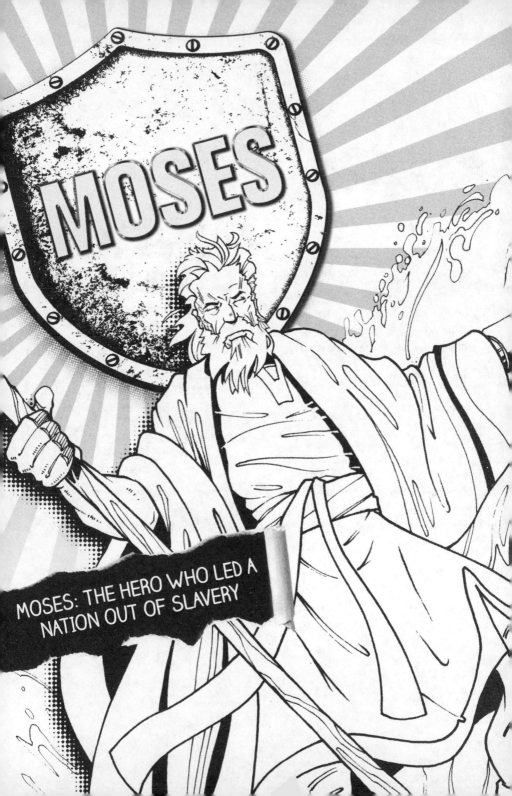

MOSES: THE HERO WHO LED A NATION OUT OF SLAVERY

A TRUE HERO FOR GOD . . . **LOVES GOD, NOT WORLDLY TREASURE.**

A HERO'S TALE

Strolling past the Great Pyramid and the Sphinx. Floating down the Nile River on a pleasure cruise. Rolling through the capital city of Thebes in a royal chariot. Marveling at his princely riches in the wealthiest, most powerful nation in the ancient world.

Wow, what a life!

As a young boy, Moses might have done all this. Israel's first great leader actually grew up in Egypt's royal palace.

At the time of Moses' birth, the reigning king, called the pharaoh, had ordered the death of all Hebrew baby boys, so Moses' parents hid him in a floating basket on the Nile River. Pharaoh's daughter saw him among the reeds and adopted him.

> ### MESSAGE FROM HEADQUARTERS
>
> DON'T STORE UP TREASURES HERE ON EARTH, WHERE MOTHS EAT THEM AND RUST DESTROYS THEM, AND WHERE THIEVES BREAK IN AND STEAL. STORE YOUR TREASURES IN HEAVEN, WHERE MOTHS AND RUST CANNOT DESTROY, AND THIEVES DO NOT BREAK IN AND STEAL. WHEREVER YOUR TREASURE IS, THERE THE DESIRES OF YOUR HEART WILL ALSO BE.
>
> – MATTHEW 6:19-21

Moses grew up in Egyptian luxury, with every conceivable pleasure in the world at his fingertips. But instead of basking in a life of riches and fame, he chose to wander around the desert and endure countless difficulties with a group of complaining Israelites.

Was he crazy?

DECODING THE MESSAGE

No, Moses wasn't crazy. In fact, he was quite the opposite. Listen to what Hebrews 11:24-26 says: "It was by faith that Moses, when he grew up, refused to be called the son of Pharaoh's daughter. He chose to share the oppression of God's people instead of enjoying the fleeting pleasures of sin. He thought it was better to suffer for the sake of Christ than to own the treasures of Egypt, for he was looking ahead to his great reward."

Moses knew that all the piles of glittering gold in the pharaohs' tombs were going to stay exactly where they were—in dusty, cobweb-filled burial chambers. Moses realized that you can't take earthly riches with you when you die.

We need to understand this too. True heroes for God know that money and earthly possessions will fade away. They understand that God created us to worship *him*, not stuff.

For those who treasure God above everything else, there's a reward that makes all the world's treasures look like a tiny piggy bank. It's a life spent in wonderful fellowship with God, both on earth and in heaven. Now *that's* true riches!

BATTLE PLAN

Ask your parents to help you set up a tithing plan for church. (*Tithing* means giving a portion of your money back to God.) It's a great way to love God, not worldly treasure.

A TRUE HERO FOR GOD . . . SAYS, "GOD, SHOW YOUR STRENGTH THROUGH MY WEAKNESS."

A HERO'S TALE

By most standards, Moses was the greatest leader in Israel's long history.

He led a million or more Israelites out of Egyptian slavery. He took them through the Red Sea, guided them through 40 years of desert wandering, and led them to the edge of the Promised Land. He saved the people from God's terrible wrath multiple times by passionately praying on their behalf. He acted as a judge for the entire nation. He stood in God's presence, received the Ten Commandments, and presented God's laws to the people.

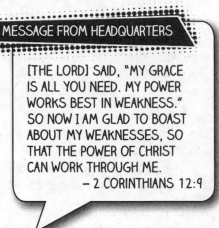

MESSAGE FROM HEADQUARTERS

[THE LORD] SAID, "MY GRACE IS ALL YOU NEED. MY POWER WORKS BEST IN WEAKNESS." SO NOW I AM GLAD TO BOAST ABOUT MY WEAKNESSES, SO THAT THE POWER OF CHRIST CAN WORK THROUGH ME.
— 2 CORINTHIANS 12:9

But to hear Moses tell it, he was a big ol' loser.

When God called Moses to free Israel from Pharaoh (see Exodus 3), Moses didn't exactly jump at the chance. Actually, Israel's future hero came up with every excuse he could *not* to go:

- "Who am I?" (Exodus 3:11)—Moses' first excuse was that he was a nobody and that no one would listen to him, certainly not a powerful king like Pharaoh.
- "I'm not very good with words" (Exodus 4:10)—Moses then claimed that he wasn't a good public speaker.
- "Lord, please! Send anyone else" (Exodus 4:13)—Moses' last excuse was just a flat-out appeal to God not to send him.

God wasn't interested in Moses' excuses, just his obedience. Reluctantly, with the help of his brother, Aaron, Moses agreed to go. And the rest, as they say, is history.

DECODING THE MESSAGE

Despite all his impressive talents and achievements later in life, Moses started as a weak, timid, sinfully reluctant man. That's good news for the rest of us because it gives us hope. If Moses can do it, so can we!

You see, when God searches for people to serve him, he doesn't look for those who are already strong heroes. He often looks for weak individuals whom he can make into heroes by his power. That way, God gets the credit, not us.

This requires humility on our part. We have to be willing to say, "God, I'm nothing without you. But please use me however you want to for your glory, not mine." Moses did that. So did the apostle Paul, who wrote today's verse, and many other heroes of the Bible. They all started off as weak, needy sinners, but by God's power, they accomplished great deeds.

God can do that through you, too!

BATTLE PLAN

Memorize 2 Corinthians 12:9 and say it as a prayer to God.

GOSPEL CONNECTION

The greatest way that God shows his amazing power in our weakness is when he forgives our sins and begins to change our rebellious hearts so that we want to obey him. This is only possible when God's Spirit works in our hearts and we put our faith in Jesus.

DAY 18

LOVES GOD AND HATES SIN.

A HERO'S TALE

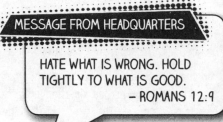

MESSAGE FROM HEADQUARTERS

HATE WHAT IS WRONG. HOLD TIGHTLY TO WHAT IS GOOD.
– ROMANS 12:9

Was Moses dead? Did he fall into a pit? Did he get attacked by a pack of angry squirrels? Did he hop on a camel and head for the nearest beach? Nobody knew.

In Exodus 32, the people of Israel had no idea what had happened to their leader. Forty days earlier, God had called Moses up Mount Sinai to receive the Ten Commandments and other laws for the nation. But there had been no sign of Moses since.

The Israelites grew impatient. So they asked Aaron to make a golden calf idol for them to worship, just like they saw when they were in Egypt. It was a terrible request because God had told them (1) they must only worship him and (2) they must not make any images to represent him.

By this time, Moses (who, yes, was still alive) had started down the mountain. But when he heard loud noises like a party from below, he looked down and saw the people worshiping the calf.

Moses, you might say, was a wee bit angry. He hurled down the Ten Commandments, smashing the stone tablets to bits at the foot of the mountain. Then he rushed to the golden calf, crushed it into powder, mixed the powder with water, and forced the Israelites to drink it. After that, he had 3,000 of the idolaters killed.

Yep, Moses was not a happy camper.

DECODING THE MESSAGE

You might be thinking, *Temper, temper, Moses!* But in this instance, Moses' anger wasn't wrong. It was directed at Israel's wickedness. Moses loved God and hated sin too much to let the people continue in their wicked ways.

We should follow Moses' example. No, we're not talking about smashing things to pieces or forcing your friends to drink bitter water. We're talking about Moses' example of loving God and hating sin. More than anything, it's an attitude of our hearts.

God isn't okay with our loving him mostly, but liking sin a little. No, God wants our *whole* hearts. Like Moses, we should passionately love God, seek to serve him, and avoid sin like it's a contagious disease.

Growing in godliness doesn't happen overnight. It's a process. The Bible calls this process "sanctification." We're not always going to do it perfectly. But as we grow to love God more and more, our desire to sin will become less and less.

BATTLE PLAN

Identify a sin you really struggle with. Maybe it's lying or being selfish or calling other people names. Then pray that God would give you the strength to overcome it.

DAY 19

FOLLOWS GOD EVEN WHEN IT'S NOT POPULAR.

A HERO'S TALE

Have you ever wondered what it would be like to be a spy? Secret missions. Clever disguises. Cool gadgets. Fast cars. How exciting! At least that's how Hollywood portrays it.

Did you know there are spy stories in the Bible, too? It's true! Numbers 13 tells about a covert Israelite operation.

> **MESSAGE FROM HEADQUARTERS**
>
> [JESUS SAID,] "IF THE WORLD HATES YOU, REMEMBER THAT IT HATED ME FIRST."
> – JOHN 15:18

God's people had reached the edge of the Promised Land. Before they entered Canaan, Moses sent 12 men ahead to spy it out. For the next 40 days, the spies secretly explored the land to prepare for their coming invasion.

But when the spies returned, 10 of them gave a bad report. They shook in fear as they recalled seeing huge fortified cities, vast enemy armies, and even giants. Conquering Canaan, they said, was "Mission: Impossible."

Only two spies, Joshua and Caleb, believed that God would keep his promise and give them victory. It was 10 against 2. What would Joshua and Caleb do? Would they give in to the pressure of the crowd? No. Joshua and Caleb begged their countrymen not to be afraid because "the LORD is with us!" (Numbers 14:9).

But the people wouldn't listen. They lost courage, talked about returning to Egypt, and even threatened to stone Joshua and Caleb!

So God punished the people for their lack of faith. For the next 40 years, he forced Israel to wander in deserts outside Canaan until the entire generation of unbelieving adults had died.

DECODING THE MESSAGE

Following God isn't always popular. Joshua and Caleb found that out firsthand. Some people might laugh at you. Others might stop being your friend. Sometimes, people even physically attack Christians because of their faith.

Worldly peer pressure can be strong, but that doesn't mean it's right. Following God is always the best thing to do.

Even Jesus faced huge peer pressure when he was on earth. The religious leaders of his day constantly fought against him. In John 15:18-25, Jesus warned his disciples to expect to have a hard time in this world. If the world hated God's own Son, he said, God's followers should expect opposition too.

But God will always bless his followers. Take Joshua and Caleb, for instance. They were the only spies who survived the 40-year desert wanderings. After Moses died, Joshua became Israel's leader, and Caleb was rewarded with a special piece of Canaanite land for his descendants.

If you follow God, he will help and bless you, too!

BATTLE PLAN

Talk to your parents and develop a plan for what to do when the crowd wants you to disobey God. Being prepared for such moments will make it easier to follow God.

DAY 20

IS STRONG AND COURAGEOUS IN THE LORD.

A HERO'S TALE

Moses was dead. The man who had led Israel out of Egypt was buried east of the Jordan River, just short of the Promised Land.

Hundreds of thousands of Israelites from the Egyptian Exodus were also gone. They had perished while wandering in the desert for 40 years—punishment for fearing the Canaanites more than trusting God.

Now, Moses' assistant, Joshua, was ready to lead Israel into the land that God had promised to Abraham hundreds of years earlier.

MESSAGE FROM HEADQUARTERS

[THE LORD SAID,] "THIS IS MY COMMAND – BE STRONG AND COURAGEOUS! DO NOT BE AFRAID OR DISCOURAGED. FOR THE LORD YOUR GOD IS WITH YOU WHEREVER YOU GO."
– JOSHUA 1:9

But Canaan was filled with mighty fortresses and powerful enemy armies. What's more, the Anakim, a scary race of giants who had frightened Israel's previous generation, still lived in the land.

Imagine how nervous Joshua must have felt. With Moses gone, the huge task of conquering Canaan fell to him.

As Joshua prepared to enter the land, God commanded him to "be strong and courageous." Fear was not allowed.

DECODING THE MESSAGE

Every hero is supposed to be strong and courageous, right? After all, when was the last time you got excited about a hero who trembles at danger? But the challenges facing Joshua were huge. Wasn't it okay to fear just a little?

Nope.

The Bible calls fear sin. Fear shows a lack of trust in God. When we give in to fear, it's like saying, "This danger or problem I'm facing is more powerful than God."

And that's a lie.

To help Joshua be strong and courageous, God reminded him of who *God* is. Check out his reminders in Joshua 1:1-9:

- God always keeps his promises (see verse 3).
- God blesses and protects his people (see verse 5).
- No one can change God's plans (see verse 5).
- God is with his people wherever they go (see verses 5 and 9).

Joshua's reasons for being strong and courageous had nothing to do with himself. They were all about who God is.

This applies to us, too. The God of Joshua's day is the same today. He still keeps his promises, loves his people, and wants to help us in all our problems.

Because of who God is, we don't have to fear. We can be strong and courageous when we trust in his unchanging character, love, and power!

BATTLE PLAN

The next time you're tempted to fear, read Joshua 1:7-9 like God is talking directly to you, because he is. Those words weren't just for Joshua. They're for you, too!

GOSPEL CONNECTION

We can be strong and courageous in the Lord because of what he has done for us through Jesus Christ. If God was willing to sacrifice his own perfect Son on the cross for us, he certainly loves us enough to help us face life's challenges!

A TRUE HERO FOR GOD . . .   OBEYS GOD EVEN WHEN IT'S HARD.

A HERO'S TALE

Joshua and the Israelites were home. Well, sort of.

God had brought them into Canaan, the Promised Land. Now, they had to fight for their territory.

Their first mission: destroy Jericho.

This was no small task. The Canaanites knew Israel was coming. So the city of Jericho was shut up as tightly as possible—nobody in, nobody out.

> ### MESSAGE FROM HEADQUARTERS
>
> YOU MUST LOVE THE LORD YOUR GOD AND ALWAYS OBEY HIS REQUIREMENTS, DECREES, REGULATIONS, AND COMMANDS.
> – DEUTERONOMY 11:1

According to archaeological evidence, ancient Jericho was huge and well fortified. It was about seven football fields long by three football fields wide. Two walls surrounded the city, and the inner one was four-and-a-half-feet thick with at least one stone tower built into it for defense.

As Israel's army of forty thousand soldiers neared, God told Joshua to do something very strange. He wanted all the soldiers and the priests to march around the city once a day for six days. Four Levites were to carry the Ark of the Covenant (a sacred chest that held the tablets with the Ten Commandments and that symbolized God's presence with his people), and seven priests were to blow trumpets as they walked. No one else was to make a sound. Then, on the seventh day, after the people marched around the city seven more times, they were all to shout as loudly as possible.

DECODING THE MESSAGE

What a strange command!

In ancient warfare, attacking armies usually laid siege to enemy cities, to starve the people inside until they surrendered, or built ramps to breach their defenses. Nobody ever won a battle by playing music!

Joshua could have responded in any number of ways:

- "God, you want me to do *what*?"
- "Why can't we fight?"
- "But God, won't they laugh at us?"

But Joshua didn't say any of those things. He just obeyed.

This was a remarkable act of faith on Joshua's part. God was asking Joshua to trust him and not in the army. Obeying God isn't always easy, but it's what we're called to do.

Joshua knew this. So on the seventh day, when all the Israelites shouted, Jericho's walls crumbled! God gave Joshua a miraculous victory because he trusted and obeyed God, even when it was hard.

When is it hardest for you to obey God? Is it when your parents ask you to do your least favorite chore? Or when all your friends are planning to do something that you know is wrong? Or when you know you should read your Bible but would rather play video games?

Whatever it is, God will give you victory, too, if you have faith and obey!

BATTLE PLAN

Read the whole story in Joshua 6. Then pray for God to help you when it's hard to obey, and he will answer!

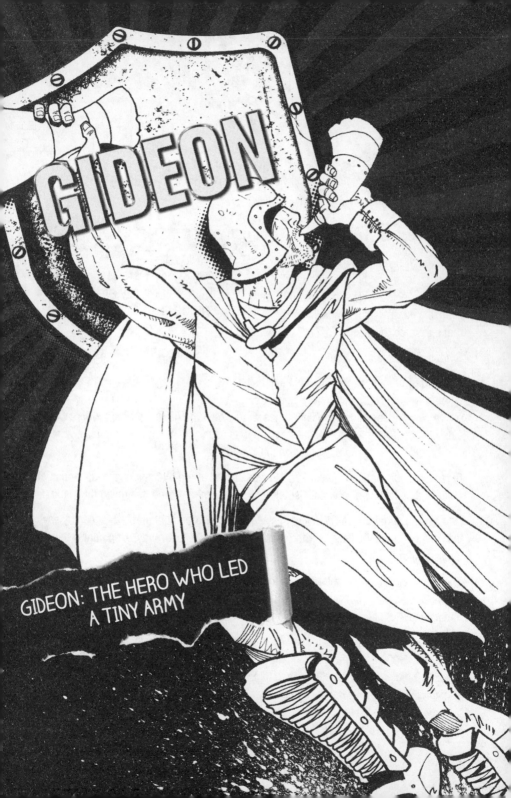

DAY 22

KNOWS THAT ALL GLORY BELONGS TO THE LORD.

A HERO'S TALE

Have you ever read a comic book about a hero hiding from the enemy? Have you ever seen a movie about a warrior trembling in a ditch? That sounds like a story that's doomed for failure!

But that's the tale of Gideon.

> **MESSAGE FROM HEADQUARTERS**
>
> ALL GLORY TO HIM WHO ALONE IS GOD, OUR SAVIOR THROUGH JESUS CHRIST OUR LORD.
> – JUDE 1:25

When we first meet Gideon in Judges 6, he's doing something odd: threshing wheat in a winepress. Winepresses in ancient times were pits in the ground where farmers would extract juice from grapes. Threshing wheat was usually done on level ground so the wind could separate the unwanted chaff from the wheat.

Gideon was hiding while he worked. He was scared of the Midianites, a nasty nation of camel-riding invaders who stole Israel's crops and animals and destroyed their land.

One day, an angel from God visited this scaredy-cat. The angel greeted Gideon by saying, "Mighty hero, the LORD is with you!" (Judges 6:12). Apparently, even angels have a sense of humor.

The angel told Gideon that God had chosen him to rescue Israel from Midian. Gideon's response was not exactly heroic. He questioned why God was allowing Israel's enemies to succeed. He made excuses. He even tested God by asking for three miracles.

Finally, Gideon agreed to obey God and lead Israel into battle against Midian's powerful army of 135,000 soldiers. Then God did something strange. He whittled Gideon's army of 32,000 men down to 300. God then told Gideon's soldiers that they were to attack Midian with trumpets, torches, and empty clay jars!

DECODING THE MESSAGE

It all sounded like a big joke. Why would God choose a fearful, unimportant man to lead a tiny army into a battle without swords?

Because it's all about glory.

The dictionary defines *glory* as "praise, honor, or distinction." It's the fame someone gets when he or she does something great.

The Bible says all glory is for God, not us. Read through God's Word and you'll see that he often calls unimportant people to do amazing things that they could never do by themselves. God loves using human weakness to show his perfect strength. When Israel needed him most, God showed them, through Gideon, that the power to save comes from God alone.

By the way, Gideon's teeny army won the battle. You can read more about it in Judges 7–8. It was a miraculous victory that could come only from the almighty God who deserves all the glory!

BATTLE PLAN

Write a list of your five greatest accomplishments:

1. _____

2. _____

3. _____

4. _____

5. _____

Now prayerfully give God glory for allowing you to achieve each one!

DAY 23

FEARS GOD, NOT MAN.

A HERO'S TALE

With God's help, Gideon won a mighty victory for Israel over the Midianites with 300 soldiers and a bunch of trumpets, torches, and empty jars. Pretty impressive! But early on, this guy didn't win any courage awards.

> ### MESSAGE FROM HEADQUARTERS
>
> I TRUST IN GOD, SO WHY SHOULD I BE AFRAID? WHAT CAN MERE MORTALS DO TO ME?
> – PSALM 56:11

We already learned that when God first called Gideon, he was hiding in a big ditch. But before Gideon fought the Midianites, God tested Gideon's courage another way. God told him to destroy his father's altar to Baal and his town's Asherah pole. Baal and Asherah were false Canaanite gods, and their idols were probably in the middle of town. If Gideon obeyed God, everyone would see what he was doing, and his father would probably get angry.

Gideon was scared. He obeyed God, but he was so afraid of the people's reactions that he destroyed the altars at nighttime.

DECODING THE MESSAGE

Following God is not always easy. Sometimes it requires us to make hard decisions. And not everyone will like us for it. In fact, the Bible warns us that the world will not be friendly toward Christians (see John 15:18-25). Gideon's fellow townspeople wanted to kill him for destroying their idols, but God saved him.

God calls us to follow him, regardless of how others treat us. We are to fear God, not people.

Today's verse asks a rhetorical question. That's a question where the reader should already know the answer. The verse says, "What can mere mortals do to me?" In other words, when it comes to obeying God, why should we fear other people? The implied answer is, "We shouldn't."

Sure, people can tease us or ignore us for following God. In some parts of the world, Christians are even threatened, thrown into jail, or killed.

But ultimately, we will answer to God, not man. People can only hurt us physically or emotionally. But God has power over our souls (see Matthew 10:28). We should live to please him, rather than worrying about what others think of us. After all, he's a loving God who takes care of his children!

BATTLE PLAN

Talk to your parents about how to respond if someone makes fun of you for following God. Develop a plan of what to say and do.

GOSPEL CONNECTION

Matthew 10:28 says, "Don't be afraid of those [that is, other people] who want to kill your body; they cannot touch your soul. Fear only God, who can destroy both soul and body in hell." That might sound harsh, but we all deserve hell because of our sins. However, Jesus came to save us from hell by dying on the cross for us!

DAY 24

BELIEVES THERE IS ONLY ONE TRUE GOD.

A HERO'S TALE

By Gideon's time, idolatry had spread through Israel like a plague. Tragically, God's people had ignored the first two commandments (see Exodus 20) and started worshiping many of the false gods of the wicked Canaanites. Even Gideon's father, Joash, was guilty of this terrible sin (see Judges 6:25).

> **MESSAGE FROM HEADQUARTERS**
>
> REMEMBER THIS AND KEEP IT FIRMLY IN MIND: THE LORD IS GOD BOTH IN HEAVEN AND ON EARTH, AND THERE IS NO OTHER.
> – DEUTERONOMY 4:39

So before God sent Gideon into battle, he wanted to prove a very important point to his unfaithful people. God told Gideon to tie one of his father's bulls to the town's Baal altar and have the bull tear it down. It's helpful to know that the symbol of Baal was often a bull. By asking Gideon to destroy Baal's altar with a live bull, God was showing his people how silly it was to worship a bull god. God also told Gideon to chop down the town's pole to Asherah, another false god, and use the wood to offer a proper sacrifice to the real God.

The next morning, when the townspeople saw their sacred idols destroyed, they were furious. They rushed to Joash's house and shouted, "Bring out your son. He must die!"

But Joash responded wisely. "If Baal really is a god," he said, "he can defend himself when someone breaks down his altar."

Baal (and Asherah) never answered, and Gideon went on to lead God's people to victory over Midian. Gideon had clearly proved that Baal and Asherah were fake gods.

DECODING THE MESSAGE

Today, no one worships Baal or Asherah anymore. But there are plenty of false gods out there.

Buddhists worship an idol named Buddha. In Hinduism, people believe in many gods. Islam speaks of worshiping God, but it's not the true God of the Bible. Those are just a few examples of false religions today. But there are plenty of others.

Scripture, including today's verse from Deuteronomy 4:39, is very clear that the God of the Bible is the only real God. True heroes for God believe that and allow it to affect how they live. Just like Gideon.

BATTLE PLAN

Tell one or more of your friends who follow another religion about the one true God. If they don't believe at first, be patient with them. Pray for them and lovingly show them Bible verses to help them believe, if they'll let you.

GOSPEL CONNECTION

There is only one true God, and his Son, Jesus Christ, is the only way to heaven. Referring to Jesus, Acts 4:12 says, "There is salvation in no one else! God has given no other name under heaven by which we must be saved."

DAY 25

A HERO'S TALE

When people talk about Bible heroes, Ruth usually isn't near the top of the list. But this quiet, godly woman was every bit the hero that famous guys like Moses, David, and Elijah were.

Ruth was from Moab, an idol-worshiping country that often fought against Israel. But at some point, she put her faith in the one true God.

Ruth had married an Israelite man named Mahlon, who had traveled to Moab with his father (Elimelech), mother (Naomi), and brother (Kilion) to escape a famine in Israel. But after more than 10 years of living in Moab, Elimelech, Mahlon, and Kilion died, leaving Naomi without a husband or son. This was bad news for Naomi. Back then, society didn't favor women having jobs (especially older women). Left alone, Naomi was in danger of going homeless and hungry.

So she decided to return to Israel, where her countrymen could support her. She told her two widowed daughters-in-law, Ruth and Orpah, to go back to their families.

But Ruth wouldn't leave Naomi. This brave young woman saw the trouble her mother-in-law was in and made one of the most beautiful promises in the Bible: "Wherever you go, I will go; wherever you live, I will live. Your people will be my people, and your God will be my God" (Ruth 1:16).

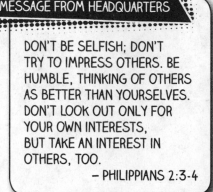

MESSAGE FROM HEADQUARTERS

DON'T BE SELFISH; DON'T TRY TO IMPRESS OTHERS. BE HUMBLE, THINKING OF OTHERS AS BETTER THAN YOURSELVES. DON'T LOOK OUT ONLY FOR YOUR OWN INTERESTS, BUT TAKE AN INTEREST IN OTHERS, TOO.
— PHILIPPIANS 2:3-4

DECODING THE MESSAGE

Ruth didn't conquer nations, part seas, or slay giants. But she was still a great hero for God. Her heroism was seen in a loving heart that put others first.

We should follow Ruth's example. Opportunities to put others first are all around us. It could be as simple as sharing your favorite toy with your sibling, or as unique as helping needy orphans in a developing country. Whatever you do, the important thing is to show godly humility by considering others better than yourself. Is it always easy? No way. But it's what God expects of his children. Pray for God to make you an others-first person!

BATTLE PLAN

Take some time you normally spend on yourself (watching TV, playing video games, etc.) and instead use it to show kindness to someone else. You might even see that person's jaw hit the floor in surprise!

GOSPEL CONNECTION

No one put others first better than Jesus. He left a perfect home in heaven to come to an evil world filled with people who hated him, all so he could die a terrible death to save us from our sins. If that isn't putting others first, nothing is!

A TRUE HERO FOR GOD . . .   HAS BEEN REDEEMED BY GOD.

A HERO'S TALE

Have your parents ever told you how they met each other? If not, you should ask them. They are often really funny stories!

Maybe your parents met in school, or at a job or a party. But they probably didn't have an experience like Ruth. She met her future husband, Boaz, while they were all hot and sweaty working in a wheat field! Not exactly romantic, huh?

> **MESSAGE FROM HEADQUARTERS**
>
> PRAISE THE LORD, THE GOD OF ISRAEL, BECAUSE HE HAS VISITED AND REDEEMED HIS PEOPLE.
>
> – LUKE 1:68

Boaz was a relative of Naomi, Ruth's mother-in-law. He was what the Bible calls a kinsman-redeemer. In Old Testament law, anytime a woman's husband died childless, it was the duty of the dead husband's brother or another relative to marry the widow, provide for her, and give her a son so the family name would continue. It was an act of redemption.

This is what Boaz did for Ruth. You can read about this wonderful tale of kindness in Ruth 2–4. And here's the best part: Obed, Boaz and Ruth's son, became the grandfather of King David, Israel's greatest king and a distant earthly ancestor to Jesus, the King of kings!

DECODING THE MESSAGE

As a kinsman-redeemer, Boaz redeemed Ruth by marrying her, giving her a son, and purchasing her dead husband's property so it stayed in the family.

The word *redeem* has several dictionary meanings:

- To buy back or repurchase
- To free from what harms (example: to free a slave from captivity by paying a ransom)
- To release from blame or debt
- To repair or restore

The story of Ruth and Boaz is a wonderful example of redemption. But it's more than just a sweet bedtime story. It ultimately points ahead to how God redeems us from slavery.

That's right—did you know you were born a slave? The Bible says we all start life as slaves to sin (see Romans 6). We owe a debt we can't pay. Without redemption—or someone purchasing our freedom at a price—we will die in our sins and face God's judgment.

That's where Jesus comes in! God's Son paid the redemption price for us by dying in our place. Now, for those who put their faith in Jesus, the definitions of *redemption* we mentioned above take on a glorious new meaning:

- God has bought us back from sin and death!
- God has freed us from captivity by paying a ransom!
- God has released us from blame and debt!
- God has repaired and restored us!

Praise God for redeeming us through Jesus!

BATTLE PLAN

Go to an Internet Bible search engine like www.biblegateway.com, enter the word *redeem*, and study the verses that talk about redemption.

A TRUE HERO FOR GOD . . .   HAS BEEN RADICALLY TRANSFORMED BY GOD.

A HERO'S TALE

When it comes to toys, there's nothing better than Transformers.

Optimus Prime, Megatron, and their mechanical pals have been around for nearly 30 years—since your parents were kids! There have been Transformer action figures, comic books, TV shows, video games, animated movies, and live-action films. Transformers have been so successful because, let's face it, what's cooler than powerful, talking robots that can transform, or change, into something else—like tractor trailers, exotic race cars, and fighter jets?

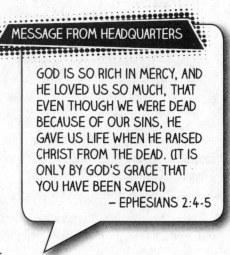

MESSAGE FROM HEADQUARTERS

GOD IS SO RICH IN MERCY, AND HE LOVED US SO MUCH, THAT EVEN THOUGH WE WERE DEAD BECAUSE OF OUR SINS, HE GAVE US LIFE WHEN HE RAISED CHRIST FROM THE DEAD. (IT IS ONLY BY GOD'S GRACE THAT YOU HAVE BEEN SAVED!)
    – EPHESIANS 2:4-5

Did you know the Bible is full of amazing stories of transformation too? It's true! Take Ruth, for example.

Ruth was from Moab, a wicked nation east of Israel. The Moabites were longtime, bitter enemies of God's people. The two countries battled on and off for more than 600 years. The Moabites worshiped many false gods and even appeared to practice child sacrifice (see 2 Kings 3:26-27).

Old Testament prophets like Isaiah, Jeremiah, Ezekiel, Amos, and Zephaniah all prophesied against Moab. And in Deuteronomy 23:3-6, the Lord himself cursed Moab and commanded Israel not to allow them into "the assembly of the LORD."

Surely God would never show love to anyone from wicked Moab, right?

Wrong.

DECODING THE MESSAGE

As we learned yesterday, the book of Ruth is a wonderful picture of redemption. But it's also a marvelous story of how God loves to transform lives.

At some point, God radically changed Ruth. He took a woman from a wicked, idol-worshiping nation and transformed her into a loving, God-fearing woman who became the great-grandmother of Israel's greatest monarch, King David, and an ancestor of Jesus himself!

By using Ruth for his purposes, God showed he can change anyone's heart. He doesn't care where we grew up or what our past is. He's in the business of transforming people from all backgrounds.

Maybe you're thinking, *That's great, but I'm not as bad as the worst Moabite.* You're probably right. But you need God's salvation just as much as the most wicked idol worshiper. The Bible says all of us were born "dead in transgressions" but that God can make us "alive with Christ" (Ephesians 2:5, NIV). Talk about a great transformation!

Has God transformed your life? It happens only if you trust in the life-changing power of Jesus' death and resurrection. When you do that, God will forgive your sins and start transforming your heart to obey him!

BATTLE PLAN

Next time you watch or play with something Transformers related, thank God for transforming lives!

SAMUEL: THE HERO WHO
ANOINTED KINGS

DAY 28

KNOWS THAT ONLY FAITH IN JESUS CAN SAVE US.

A HERO'S TALE

Samuel was a special kid.

He was a miraculous gift from God to his parents, who couldn't have children on their own. When Samuel was still very young, his mother dedicated him to the Lord's service at the tabernacle, the large tent where Israel worshiped and sacrificed to God before King Solomon built the temple.

Samuel spent his entire childhood serving Eli, the high priest, and the Lord at the tabernacle. Later in life, he became one of Israel's greatest prophets and anointed Israel's first two kings at God's command. If anybody could earn God's favor, it would be Samuel, right?

> ## MESSAGE FROM HEADQUARTERS
>
> GOD SAVED YOU BY HIS GRACE WHEN YOU BELIEVED. AND YOU CAN'T TAKE CREDIT FOR THIS; IT IS A GIFT FROM GOD. SALVATION IS NOT A REWARD FOR THE GOOD THINGS WE HAVE DONE, SO NONE OF US CAN BOAST ABOUT IT.
>
> – EPHESIANS 2:8-9

But in 1 Samuel 3—the story of God calling Samuel in the middle of the night—the Bible mentions something interesting: "Samuel did not yet know the LORD because he had never had a message from the LORD before" (verse 7).

DECODING THE MESSAGE

Whoa! Wait a minute. How is it possible that Samuel didn't know the Lord yet? Samuel's parents had dedicated him to the Lord before he was out of diapers. Every day, Samuel served in God's tabernacle. Didn't he have special privileges with God or something?

Nope.

This is a small part of Samuel's life story, but it's very important to understand. In ancient Israel, many Israelites believed they automatically earned God's favor because of their heritage (that they were Israelites) or the good things they did. Lots of people believe the same thing today. But as Samuel's story shows, truly knowing God isn't a matter of race, upbringing, or human effort.

Nothing we do can save us or earn God's favor. No amount of good works can do it. Neither can attending church every Sunday or growing up in a Christian home.

Because of our sin, we are separated from God and need help. But God's forgiveness isn't earned—it's a gift (see today's verse). And that gift is God's Son, Jesus. He died to save us.

As Samuel grew older, he trusted in the Lord, and God gave him the gift of salvation. (Even though Samuel lived long before Jesus came to earth and died for our sins, he believed that God would one day send a Savior [see Hebrews 11:13].) A true hero for God understands that only faith in Jesus can save him or her. Have you trusted in God's saving Son?

BATTLE PLAN

Make a list of everything good you've ever done. (It can be as long as you want.) Don't read any further until you do this. . . . Finished? Good. Now crumple up the paper and throw it away as a reminder that doing good things can't save you—only Jesus can!

A TRUE HERO FOR GOD . . .   ANSWERS GOD'S CALL ON HIS LIFE.

A HERO'S TALE

Have you ever heard voices in the night? Scary!

Okay, maybe you won't admit to being scared of the dark. But plenty of kids are. Either way, it's certainly no fun to hear strange noises in bed.

MESSAGE FROM HEADQUARTERS

IF HE CALLS YOU, SAY, "SPEAK, LORD, FOR YOUR SERVANT IS LISTENING."
— 1 SAMUEL 3:9, NIV

Well, that's exactly what happened to little Samuel. One night, when Samuel was a young boy serving in the tabernacle, he heard a mysterious voice say his name. What would you have done? Hidden under the covers? Run screaming out of the room? Slowly reached for your lightsaber?

Samuel didn't do any of that (lightsabers, of course, hadn't been invented yet). He jumped out of bed and ran to Eli, the high priest, thinking Eli had called him.

But Eli hadn't said a word. This happened two more times. Finally, Eli realized it was the Lord's voice calling Samuel. He told Samuel to lie down and gave him instructions in case he heard the voice again.

A few moments later, the voice returned. "Samuel! Samuel!" it called. Samuel rose from his bed and responded like Eli had told him to. "Speak, Lord, for your servant is listening," he said.

Then, God gave Samuel a difficult task: he told Samuel to tell Eli that Eli's two sons would soon be punished without mercy for living wicked lives. Imagine having to tell a message like that to an important, powerful leader of your country who had been raising you since you were a toddler. That was the situation Samuel faced.

Amazingly, little Samuel faithfully obeyed God and eventually grew up to become one of Israel's greatest prophets.

DECODING THE MESSAGE

God called Samuel in a unique way. But even today, thousands of years later, God still calls each of us to follow him (even though we might not be in our pajamas when he does). Maybe he's calling you now, through this devotional book.

First, God calls us to put our trust in his Son, Jesus, for the forgiveness of our sins. Then, when we become his children through faith, he calls us to obey him and use our talents to serve him.

Samuel became a courageous prophet. What is God calling you to do? What talents is he calling you to use for his glory?

Whenever God calls you, make sure you respond like Samuel: "Speak, Lord, for your servant is listening!"

BATTLE PLAN

Ask your parents and others close to you what they think you're good at. This could be a great first step at identifying what God's calling on your life is.

A TRUE HERO FOR GOD . . . DOESN'T USE AGE AS AN EXCUSE.

A HERO'S TALE

Has your mom or dad ever dropped you off at school or soccer practice or your grandma's house? It's always nice to see your parents again when they pick you up, isn't it? But imagine if they dropped you off and returned to see you only once a year. Yikes!

That's exactly what happened to Samuel. He was just a little pip-squeak—maybe only three or four years old—when his parents left him with Eli, Israel's high priest, and returned home. They did this to fulfill a promise that his mother, Hannah, had made to God before she was able to give birth (see 1 Samuel 1:11).

> ### MESSAGE FROM HEADQUARTERS
>
> DON'T LET ANYONE THINK LESS OF YOU BECAUSE YOU ARE YOUNG. BE AN EXAMPLE TO ALL BELIEVERS IN WHAT YOU SAY, IN THE WAY YOU LIVE, IN YOUR LOVE, YOUR FAITH, AND YOUR PURITY.
> – 1 TIMOTHY 4:12

Little Samuel faithfully served the Lord in the tabernacle during his childhood. As Samuel grew older, God made him a powerful prophet who led the entire nation of Israel before Israel had any kings. Eventually, Samuel crowned Israel's first two rulers, Saul and David.

Samuel was a pretty important guy. And it all started when he was a kid.

DECODING THE MESSAGE

Have you ever been told, "This is only for adults"? Or "You can do that when you're older"?

Sometimes, it's no fun to be a kid! Can't eat whatever you want. Can't drive. Forced to sit at the kid table at large family gatherings. Always told what to do. Gotta do homework every night. Told to go to bed at a certain time.

Sheesh. Can't a kid do anything cool?

Yes, kids can do great things for God! For proof, look no further than the life of Samuel. He started doing great things for God when he was only a boy.

In fact, the Bible shares plenty of stories about superkids besides Samuel. David killed Goliath when he was "little more than a boy" (1 Samuel 17:42, NIV). Joash was seven when he became king of Judah (see 2 Kings 11:21), and Josiah was eight when he began to rule (see 2 Kings 22:1). Jeremiah thought he was "too young" when God called him to become a prophet (see Jeremiah 1:6). And don't forget the little boy who generously gave up his lunch to help Jesus feed 5,000 people (see John 6:9).

True heroes for God don't use age as an excuse. Age doesn't matter to God. All you need is faith in him and a willing heart, and he can use you in mighty ways!

BATTLE PLAN

Ask your parents to help you find a ministry at church or in the community where you can start serving the Lord right now, no matter how young you are!

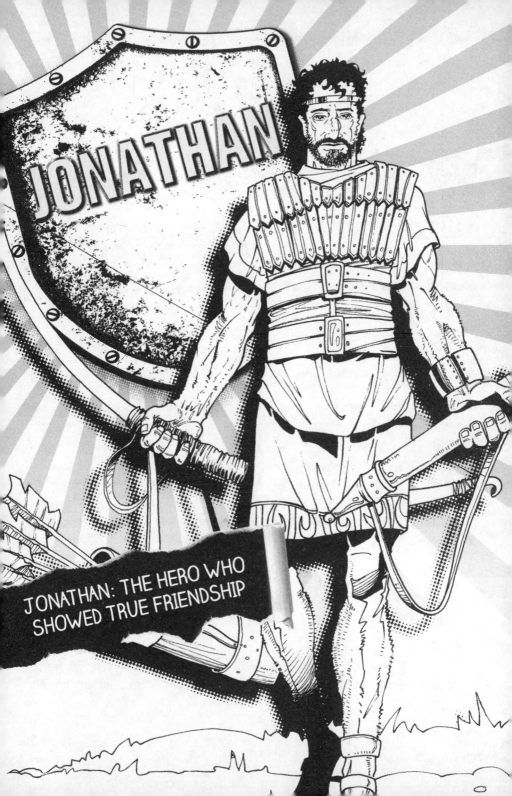

DAY 31

A HERO'S TALE

Israel was in trouble.

God had rejected Saul, Israel's first king, for his disobedience, and the young nation was at war with Philistia. The Philistines had gained control of all the blacksmiths in Canaan, meaning the Israelites had no way of making metal weapons to defend themselves. The Bible says, "Not a soldier with Saul and Jonathan had a sword or spear in his hand; only Saul and his son Jonathan had them" (1 Samuel 13:22, NIV).

> **MESSAGE FROM HEADQUARTERS**
>
> BE STRONG AND COURAGEOUS! DO NOT BE AFRAID AND DO NOT PANIC BEFORE THEM. FOR THE LORD YOUR GOD WILL PERSONALLY GO AHEAD OF YOU. HE WILL NEITHER FAIL YOU NOR ABANDON YOU.
>   – DEUTERONOMY 31:6

Worse yet, Saul's standing army was only 600 men, while the Philistines boasted thousands of chariots and "as many warriors as the grains of sand on the seashore" (1 Samuel 13:5). Israel's situation was so desperate that many soldiers deserted Saul and joined the enemy. Others hid in any cave or hole they could find. With a clear military advantage, the Philistines were tightening their grip on central Israel.

Jonathan, Saul's son, had every reason to be scared. As the crown prince of Israel, his future kingdom seemed to be slipping away. He could've retreated to the palace, trembling in fear. Or he could've hid in a nearby cave with others.

But he didn't.

With great courage, Jonathan and his armor bearer climbed up a rocky cliff, attacked a Philistine outpost, and killed 20 men by themselves. When Philistia's main army found out, the soldiers panicked and started fighting each other. Saul heard of this and took advantage of his enemy's weakness. (Check out the whole story in 1 Samuel 14.)

Jonathan's bravery sparked a great Israelite victory!

DECODING THE MESSAGE

Putting 2 against 20 isn't very good odds. Would you and a friend ever go up against 20 nasty neighborhood bullies? No way!

But Jonathan didn't think twice about it. This swashbuckling hero was one courageous dude. Listen to what he told his armor bearer before they attacked: "Nothing can hinder the LORD. He can win a battle whether he has many warriors or only a few!" (1 Samuel 14:6).

Did you notice where Jonathan's courage came from? It wasn't his own strength or fighting skills. It came from his trust in the Lord.

God is fully trustworthy because he is all-powerful and all-knowing—and he loves you. He protects his children and does only what's best for them.

The same God who loved and helped Jonathan also loves and wants to help you. No matter what difficult situation you're facing, take courage in the Lord. He is fully trustworthy!

BATTLE PLAN

Memorize today's verse as a helpful reminder for times when you need courage. If you want other similar verses, check out Joshua 1:9 and 1 Corinthians 16:13.

DAY 32

A HERO'S TALE

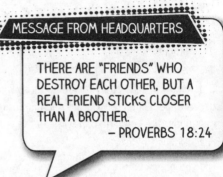

MESSAGE FROM HEADQUARTERS

THERE ARE "FRIENDS" WHO DESTROY EACH OTHER, BUT A REAL FRIEND STICKS CLOSER THAN A BROTHER.
— PROVERBS 18:24

Jonathan had every reason to dislike David.

The young shepherd boy from Bethlehem had literally become an overnight hero in Israel when he killed Goliath the giant and sparked a huge military victory over the Philistines. Instantly, the whole country was talking about David. Women sang songs about him. Older men respected him. Everybody seemed to love him.

Except King Saul. Jonathan's father grew jealous of David and became consumed with hatred toward him. Saul tried to kill David many times. In Saul's mind, David was getting all the attention Saul should've been receiving, and he represented a threat to Saul's rule.

Jonathan had become friends with David after the victory over Goliath. But as things started unfolding, Jonathan could have sided with his father. After all, as prince of Israel, Jonathan was the natural heir to Saul's throne. He could have very easily turned against David and sought David's harm to protect his own future reign as king.

But that's not what Jonathan did. He was a faithful friend. As a sign of love and friendship, he gave David some of his royal clothing, as well as his sword and bow. (You can read about their friendship in 1 Samuel 18–20.)

Jonathan remained so loyal to David that Saul even tried to kill his own son. When Saul was hunting for David, Jonathan secretly came to David to encourage him, at the risk of his own life. Later, Jonathan willingly surrendered his claim to the throne for David.

Jonathan was an incredibly brave and faithful friend!

DECODING THE MESSAGE

What kind of friend are you? Are you someone who is more concerned with yourself or with others? Do you speak kindly to those around you? Can you be trusted?

If you want to be a faithful friend, you should

- always put others first;
- be trustworthy;
- look for ways to bless others;
- speak kindly to everyone;
- willingly share with others;
- be there to listen to others or help them in their time of need;
- stand up for others when the crowd is against them; and
- be joyful, not jealous, when good things happen to others.

Today's verse talks about the benefits of close friendship. You'll never regret being that type of friend to others.

It's not easy to be a faithful friend. It takes lots of work and prayer to overcome our sinful, selfish desires. But with God's help, you can do it!

BATTLE PLAN

Pray through the "faithful friend" list above and ask God to help you become this type of friend.

DAY 33

LOVES OTHERS AS HIMSELF.

A HERO'S TALE

The story of Jonathan and David is one of the greatest tales of friendship in the Bible.

When the Bible describes their bond, it uses an interesting phrase. It says Jonathan "loved [David] as he loved himself" (1 Samuel 18:3). In fact, 1 Samuel uses this phrase three different times to describe Jonathan's affection for his best friend. In other words, Jonathan would've done anything for David.

We see Jonathan's love for his friend in many ways in 1 Samuel:

> **MESSAGE FROM HEADQUARTERS**
>
> JESUS REPLIED, "'YOU MUST LOVE THE LORD YOUR GOD WITH ALL YOUR HEART, ALL YOUR SOUL, AND ALL YOUR MIND.' THIS IS THE FIRST AND GREATEST COMMANDMENT. A SECOND IS EQUALLY IMPORTANT: 'LOVE YOUR NEIGHBOR AS YOURSELF.'"
> – MATTHEW 22:37-39

- Jonathan shared his belongings with David and honored him (see 18:4).
- He spoke kindly about David to his father, King Saul, and tried to protect David from Saul's jealous anger (see 19:4-5).
- He was willing to do anything for David (see 20:4).
- He provided spiritual encouragement to David in a time of great need (see 23:15-18).
- He humbly acknowledged that David would be the next king of Israel instead of him (see 23:17).
- He risked his own life at least twice for David (see 20:33; 23:15-18).

Jonathan truly loved David as himself!

DECODING THE MESSAGE

We are very good at loving ourselves, aren't we? From the moment we wake up each morning, we are concerned about ourselves—what we'll eat, how we look, what we'll do that day, etc. We are usually our own favorite subject!

But the Bible calls us to something greater than self-love. When we focus only on ourselves, that's sinful pride and selfishness. When we focus on others, that's Christlike love. We are to devote as much care and attention to others as we do to ourselves.

Following God is all about humility—or not thinking too highly of ourselves. God calls us to put him first, others second, and ourselves a distant third, just like today's verse says.

A true hero for God isn't a me-first person; a hero is an others-first person!

BATTLE PLAN

Make a list of the things you like best. It can be gifts or activities or compliments you enjoy. Now give those things to a friend or sibling. It's a great way to love that person as yourself!

GOSPEL CONNECTION

The greatest example of loving others is Jesus. There's no greater love than to give up your life for someone else. Jesus loved us so much that he died the death we deserved to pay for our sins and make us right with God.

DAY 34

IS MORE CONCERNED WITH HIS HEART THAN HIS OUTWARD APPEARANCE.

A HERO'S TALE

Israel needed a new king.

Saul, the nation's first monarch, looked good at the start. He was tall, handsome, and strong, and he led Israel to many military victories. But Saul continually disobeyed God, so God rejected him.

God sent the prophet Samuel to Bethlehem to pick a new king from the eight sons of a man named Jesse (see 1 Samuel 16). One by one, Jesse's seven oldest sons passed before Samuel. He was particularly impressed with Eliab, the firstborn, who had a kingly look. But God said no to Eliab—and all the rest, too.

> **MESSAGE FROM HEADQUARTERS**
>
> BUT THE LORD SAID TO SAMUEL, "DON'T JUDGE BY HIS APPEARANCE OR HEIGHT, FOR I HAVE REJECTED HIM. THE LORD DOESN'T SEE THINGS THE WAY YOU SEE THEM. PEOPLE JUDGE BY OUTWARD APPEARANCE, BUT THE LORD LOOKS AT THE HEART."
> – 1 SAMUEL 16:7

Finally, Samuel asked Jesse if he had any other sons. "The youngest," Jesse said. "He is watching the sheep."

"Bring him," Samuel commanded. So Jesse sent for young David.

But how could David be God's chosen king? To the human eye, he wasn't special. He was the youngest brother in a culture that heavily favored the oldest. He was only a shepherd—a dirty, lowly profession. And he wasn't even important enough to be initially invited to Samuel's king-picking party!

But when David arrived, God told Samuel, "Anoint him. This is the one."

While no one else saw value in David, God saw his heart. It was a heart that trusted God.

DECODING THE MESSAGE

Did you know that Americans spend about $20 billion on cosmetic products, $33 billion on dietary products, and $300 million on cosmetic surgery each year? That's a lot of money to look good.

There's nothing wrong with wanting to look nice. After all, no one wants to be around a slob. But God cares about something far more important than outward appearance. He is most concerned with our hearts. That's why God rejected Saul as king and chose David. Saul's heart was self-centered and sinful, but David was a man after God's own heart (see 1 Samuel 13:14). In other words, David had a heart that cared about others and wanted to obey God. That kind of heart pleases God.

May God help you care less about your outward appearance and more about your heart!

BATTLE PLAN

Make sure you spend more time reading God's Word and praying each morning than you spend in front of the mirror!

GOSPEL CONNECTION

As sinners, we need Jesus' help to make us people after God's own heart. Through our faith in Jesus' sacrificial death on the cross for us, God will forgive us and transform our hearts to obey him.

DAY 35

TRUSTS IN GOD, NO MATTER WHAT THE ODDS ARE.

A HERO'S TALE

David's eyes kept going up . . . up . . . up. Was there no end to the massive man standing before him?

Goliath was a big, scary dude.

Israel was at war with Philistia, and each morning, Goliath, the Philistines' colossal champion, had dared Israel's camp to send one soldier to face him in a winner-takes-all battle. But the Israelites wanted nothing to do with the nasty giant.

> **MESSAGE FROM HEADQUARTERS**
>
> [DAVID SAID TO GOLIATH,] "EVERYONE ASSEMBLED HERE WILL KNOW THAT THE LORD RESCUES HIS PEOPLE, BUT NOT WITH SWORD AND SPEAR. THIS IS THE LORD'S BATTLE, AND HE WILL GIVE YOU TO US!"
> – 1 SAMUEL 17:47

Standing at nine feet nine inches, Goliath was taller than most grizzly bears are on their hind legs! He was a powerful warrior and a trained killer whose frightening armor and weaponry made him look like an ancient Iron Man. One glance at Goliath, and the hearts of Israel's soldiers turned into Jell-O.

Then along came David. He had arrived at the battle scene to check on his three oldest brothers, who were soldiers. But when David heard Goliath's taunts against Israel—and God—*he* volunteered to fight Goliath.

The Israelite soldiers momentarily stopped biting their nails in fear to enjoy a good laugh. How could this puny little shepherd boy hope to beat mighty Goliath? David probably stood no higher than Goliath's belly button. From all appearances, the odds were stacked against David.

But that didn't stop him. Armed with nothing but a slingshot, a few small stones, and a big trust in God, David ran toward Goliath, twirled his slingshot, and let a stone fly.

The rock smacked Goliath right between the eyes, sending the powerful giant crashing to the ground. Amazingly, David had won the battle and saved Israel! (See 1 Samuel 17 for the full story.)

DECODING THE MESSAGE

Despite his youth and size, David courageously believed the odds of victory were 100 percent in *his* favor. Why? Because David knew he had an invincible ally: God.

David understood that God is the eternal Creator and Sustainer of the universe, who can do anything that pleases him. While Goliath looked gigantic to the Israelites, he was no match for the Lord God Almighty.

We are called to display David-like trust in the Lord too. God is bigger than any enemy or problem you'll face. Whatever your challenge is, don't fear, worry, or try to fix it by yourself. Just trust in God through prayer and faith, and watch him work mightily to give you victory!

BATTLE PLAN

Read Psalm 144, which David wrote as a reminder of God's power and majesty in difficult times.

DAY 36

SEEKS GOD'S GLORY, NOT HIS OWN.

A HERO'S TALE

Once a nobody, David was now a national hero.

The young, slingshot-wielding shepherd boy from Bethlehem had killed Goliath, the mightiest warrior in Palestine, and sparked a great Israelite victory over the hated Philistines. News of David's heroism spread like wildfire. Everywhere David went, people heaped praise on him.

MESSAGE FROM HEADQUARTERS

WHETHER YOU EAT OR DRINK, OR WHATEVER YOU DO, DO IT ALL FOR THE GLORY OF GOD.
— 1 CORINTHIANS 10:31

King Saul's daughter Michal fell in love with David, and he quickly became best friends with Jonathan, Israel's prince. David was an overnight celebrity.

His popularity was so great that Saul became jealous, especially when the king heard the songs people were singing. As Saul's army traveled home after the victory over Goliath and the Philistines, Israelite women came out into the streets singing this tune:

Saul has killed his thousands,
and David his ten thousands! (1 Samuel 18:7)

(If ancient Israel had radio stations, it certainly would've become a Top 40 hit.)

After Saul died, David became Israel's greatest king, and his success continued. He subdued his enemies, greatly expanded Israel's borders, and captured Jerusalem as his new capital city.

With all his success, David very easily could've turned arrogant. He could've become addicted to his own fame and started living for his own honor.

But he didn't.

During his 40-year reign, David lived for *God's* glory. He brought the Ark of the Covenant into Jerusalem and hoped to build a temple for God (although the Lord instructed David's son Solomon to do it). David also worshiped God through music and writing. He penned at least half the book of Psalms and commanded that worship music be played frequently at the tabernacle.

Was David perfect? Certainly not. But he lived his life for God's glory, not his own.

DECODING THE MESSAGE

David is a prime example of today's verse, 1 Corinthians 10:31. God gives each of us many gifts and abilities, and he wants us to use them for his glory.

Living for our own glory is prideful, shortsighted, and sinful. God didn't create us so *we* would receive praise. He created us so we would praise *him*.

It's not always easy to honor someone else, but this is what God calls us to do. No matter what you're good at—music, sports, art, writing, science, building things, and so on—use your skills to glorify the Lord.

Do things that please God, and then give him the credit. After all, he deserves it!

BATTLE PLAN

Get in the habit of honoring God publicly and thanking him privately for the good things you do.

SOLOMON

SOLOMON: THE RICH, WISE, TEMPLE-BUILDING HERO

A TRUE HERO FOR GOD . . .   **DESIRES GODLY WISDOM.**

A HERO'S TALE

Imagine that God gave you one wish and you could ask for anything in the world. What would it be?

- A million dollars?
- Superhero powers?
- Every single video game in existence?
- A lifetime supply of Brussels sprouts? (Just kidding.)

Wow, that would be incredible, wouldn't it? Well, that's exactly what happened to King Solomon.

> ## MESSAGE FROM HEADQUARTERS
>
> FEAR OF THE LORD IS THE FOUNDATION OF TRUE KNOWLEDGE, BUT FOOLS DESPISE WISDOM AND DISCIPLINE.
>
> – PROVERBS 1:7

When Solomon first took over Israel's throne after his father, David, died, God came to him in a dream one night and said, "What do you want? Ask, and I will give it to you!" (1 Kings 3:5). What an amazing opportunity! Solomon could've asked for anything— money, power, fame, long life, the destruction of his enemies, etc. Instead, he asked for wisdom. "Give me the wisdom and knowledge to lead [my people] properly," Solomon said in 2 Chronicles 1:10, "for who could possibly govern this great people of yours?"

God was so pleased with Solomon's request, he not only granted it but also lavished him with immeasurable riches. "King Solomon became richer and wiser than any other king on earth. People from every nation came to consult him and to hear the wisdom God had given him" (1 Kings 10:23-24).

DECODING THE MESSAGE

Solomon possessed great godly wisdom. But not all wisdom is godly. The Bible warns us about worldly wisdom, which doesn't acknowledge God's existence or care about obeying him (see 1 Corinthians 1). That kind of wisdom isn't really wisdom at all. It's the worst kind of foolishness—and it eventually leads to spiritual death.

As today's verse says, the first step in being truly wise is "fearing the Lord," or submitting your life to him.

Godly wisdom

- acknowledges that God made the universe;
- knows that God is in charge, and we're not;
- understands that we were made to worship God with our lives;
- admits that we desperately need a Savior because our sins separate us from God;
- believes the only way for us to be right with God is to turn from our sins and trust in God's perfect Son, Jesus, who died on the cross to take away our punishment; and
- believes that we should live according to the Bible, God's holy Word.

So get smart! Be a true hero for God who pursues godly wisdom.

BATTLE PLAN

Putting God's Word in your heart will help you gain godly wisdom, so start a Bible memorization plan. There are lots of different ones out there. Ask your parents to help you pick one that's best for you.

A TRUE HERO FOR GOD . . .   HONORS AND OBEYS HIS PARENTS.

A HERO'S TALE

King Solomon was filthy rich.

He was virtually tripping over gold in Jerusalem (see 1 Kings 10:14-22). But he was also an incredibly wise ruler. In fact, he wrote several of the Bible's "wisdom books," such as Proverbs and Ecclesiastes. The book of Proverbs, in particular, is filled with godly wisdom. Its 31 chapters are chock-full of golden treasures of biblical knowledge.

> **MESSAGE FROM HEADQUARTERS**
>
> CHILDREN, ALWAYS OBEY YOUR PARENTS, FOR THIS PLEASES THE LORD.
> – COLOSSIANS 3:20

Of all the wise sayings Solomon could've chosen to begin Proverbs, check out what he wrote: "My child, listen when your father corrects you. Don't neglect your mother's instruction. What you learn from them will crown you with grace and be a chain of honor around your neck" (Proverbs 1:8-9).

Solomon, the wisest man on earth, who wrote more than 4,000 songs and proverbs (see 1 Kings 4:29-34), considered honoring and obeying one's parents to be of the highest importance.

DECODING THE MESSAGE

"Yes, Mom." "Yes, Dad."

Those four words are each one syllable, even possible for two-year-olds to pronounce. Yet they are four of the hardest words to say in the English language!

It's no secret—obeying your parents isn't always easy. Do you know why? It's because you have a sin problem. From the moment you were born, your heart was naturally bent against God. And if it's tough to obey your Creator, it will be tough to obey your parents, too.

If you've ever been around toddlers who are learning to speak, you've probably heard them say, "No!" to their parents. (Maybe one of those toddlers is your younger sibling!) Do you think their parents taught them to do that? No, of course not! Children's sinful desire to rebel was born inside them.

In his infinite wisdom, God has given you parents to love you and protect you. But they are also there to train you in godliness. After all, how can you obey God (whom you can't see) if you can't obey your parents (whom you *can* see)?

In fact, obeying your parents is so important that God included it as one of the Ten Commandments, right up there with "Worship God only," "Don't steal," and "Don't murder." Exodus 20:12 says, "Honor your father and mother. Then you will live a long, full life in the land the LORD your God is giving you."

Your parents are a wonderful blessing from God! Solomon, the wisest of kings, understood how important it is to obey parents. You should understand that too.

BATTLE PLAN

When your parents tell you to do something, get into the habit of saying, "Yes, Mom" or "Yes, Dad" right away. It's a great way to start obeying!

A TRUE HERO FOR GOD . . .　　WORSHIPS GOD ALONE.

A HERO'S TALE

So who was the greatest ruler in ancient Israel? Early in his 40-year reign, King Solomon appeared to have the inside track.

MESSAGE FROM HEADQUARTERS

[GOD SAID,] "YOU MUST NOT HAVE ANY OTHER GOD BUT ME."
– EXODUS 20:3

After David's wars, Solomon brought peace to Israel and enlarged the nation's borders to their greatest extent. He doubled the size of Jerusalem, built a royal palace, and fortified towns throughout the country.

Solomon's unmatched wisdom and wealth were legendary, attracting visitors from all over the world. He wrote Ecclesiastes, Song of Songs, and most of Proverbs. Most important, he built a magnificent temple for the Lord in Jerusalem.

Solomon was the man!

Sadly, though, the story of Solomon ended on a sour note. The same king who wrote that "God is the one you must fear" (Ecclesiastes 5:7, ESV) started worshiping other gods.

Throughout his life, Solomon married 700 women (whoa!), and many of them were from wicked, idol-worshiping nations around Israel. This was a direct violation of God's commands. Then "as Solomon grew old, his wives turned his heart after other gods, and his heart was not fully devoted to the LORD his God" (1 Kings 11:4, NIV). Solomon worshiped at least three false gods—Ashtoreth (of Sidon), Molech (of Ammon), and Chemosh (of Moab)—and even built altars for some of them outside Jerusalem.

God punished Solomon's unfaithfulness by causing his kingdom to split into two nations—Israel and Judah—after his death. It was a tragic ending to a promising start.

DECODING THE MESSAGE

Nobody worships Ashtoreth, Molech, or Chemosh these days. But even now, people around the world believe in many different religions and gods. Some people even think that they themselves are gods!

However, the God of the Bible is the only true God, and he calls us to worship him alone. All other gods are fakes. They're man-made phonies.

In Exodus 20:3, God directed Israel in the first of the Ten Commandments, "You must not have any other god but me." And in Isaiah 46:9, God reminded his people, "I alone am God! I am God, and there is none like me."

Why should we believe this? Because the Bible says so, and God's Word is truth. This calls for great faith from God's true heroes. Many people will disagree with you. Are you willing to answer God's call and worship him alone?

BATTLE PLAN

Read Deuteronomy 4:1-40. It's all about worshiping only God.

GOSPEL CONNECTION

Believing that the God of the Bible is the only real God is so important. But that's not enough to become a true follower of God. The Bible says that we must also put our faith in Jesus Christ, God's perfect Son, because "there is salvation in no one else! God has given no other name under heaven by which we must be saved" (Acts 4:12).

A TRUE HERO FOR GOD . . .   TRUSTS GOD FOR ALL HIS NEEDS.

A HERO'S TALE

Every good hero has an archenemy. For Elijah, the godly Old Testament prophet, it was Ahab, a wicked king who plunged Israel into worse idolatry than any king before him.

In 1 Kings 17, Elijah publicly condemned Ahab's worship of the Canaanite deity Baal and other false gods, and he told Ahab of God's punishment: for the next several years, no rain would fall on Israel until Elijah gave the word. Not even a single dewdrop. It was a terrible judgment for a nation like Israel, whose economy depended on farming.

> ### MESSAGE FROM HEADQUARTERS
>
> [PAUL SAID,] "THIS SAME GOD WHO TAKES CARE OF ME WILL SUPPLY ALL YOUR NEEDS FROM HIS GLORIOUS RICHES, WHICH HAVE BEEN GIVEN TO US IN CHRIST JESUS."
>
> – PHILIPPIANS 4:19

Ahab was furious—so furious that he tried to kill Elijah. So God sent Elijah to the Kerith Ravine, a dry, deserted area east of the Jordan River. Elijah probably wondered why God was sending him there. But he trusted God to meet his needs.

And then, something strange happened. The next morning, some ravens—those jet-black, croaking birds that often pick at dead animals—started landing near Elijah. They hopped over to him, dropped meat and bread at his feet, and flew away. They did this morning and night for many days.

Elijah also found a nearby brook to drink from. While other water sources dried up in the drought, the Kerith brook kept providing refreshment for Elijah.

The ravens and the brook were no coincidences. They were provision from the Lord. Even in a dry, remote wilderness, God met all of Elijah's needs.

DECODING THE MESSAGE

Today, almost 3,000 years after Elijah lived, God is still in the business of providing for his children's needs. But let's get something straight: the latest Xbox and PlayStation are *not* our basic needs! Neither are the other hottest new toys, movies, or Air Jordans. Our basic needs are food, water, clothing, and shelter.

God doesn't always give us what we *want*, but he always gives us what we *need*. Today's verse from Philippians 4 reminds us of that. So do Jesus' words from Matthew 6:25-34, where he told his listeners to consider how God feeds birds each day and clothes flowers with beauty. If God does that for insignificant things like birds and flowers, how much more will he take care of us, who are made in his image?

So don't worry about the necessities of life. God loves you and he will take care of all your needs. He's been doing it since life began.

BATTLE PLAN

Memorize Philippians 4:19 and read Matthew 6:25-34. They show God's care for his children.

GOSPEL CONNECTION

As important as food, water, clothing, and shelter are, none of those is our greatest need. Our greatest need is a Savior for our sins. God provided that, too, in Jesus!

DAY 41

A TRUE HERO FOR GOD . . .   **BELIEVES IN THE POWER OF PRAYER.**

A HERO'S TALE

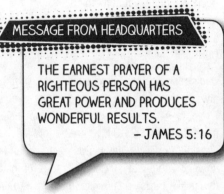

MESSAGE FROM HEADQUARTERS

THE EARNEST PRAYER OF A
RIGHTEOUS PERSON HAS
GREAT POWER AND PRODUCES
WONDERFUL RESULTS.
– JAMES 5:16

The time had almost come for rain.

But before God ended the long drought on Israel, he wanted to prove something to evil King Ahab; his wicked wife, Jezebel; and all the confused people in Israel who believed that Baal was a real god. So in 1 Kings 18, he told Elijah to gather the 450 prophets of Baal on Mount Carmel. An epic cosmic duel was about to begin.

The rules were simple: each side would sacrifice a bull on an altar. Ahab's prophets would sacrifice to Baal, and Elijah would sacrifice to God. Whoever answered with fire from heaven would prove to be the true God.

For most of the day, the false prophets shouted, danced, and even cut themselves to get Baal's attention. Not so smart, huh? Of course, nothing happened.

Finally, it was Elijah's turn. He stepped forward and busted out his secret weapon: prayer to the Lord God Almighty!

"O LORD, God of Abraham, Isaac, and Jacob," Elijah prayed, "prove today that you are God in Israel and that I am your servant" (1 Kings 18:36). Immediately, fire fell from heaven and consumed the entire altar, including a trench filled with water that Elijah had dug around it. It was a blowout victory for God!

Elijah accomplished many other great things in his life through prayer. After the God versus Baal showdown, Elijah prayed for God to end the 3½-year drought, and God sent a huge rainstorm. Another time, Elijah prayed for God to raise a widow's son from the dead, and God did.

DECODING THE MESSAGE

Was Elijah a magician? Did he possess rare superpowers? No, Elijah was simply a lean, mean praying machine!

Every great deed of Elijah's came through prayer to the one true God. When Elijah wanted to do something amazing, he always asked the Lord for help.

Prayer is simply talking to God. And it's a wonderful privilege. Sinners like us don't deserve to speak to a holy God, but that's exactly what he allows us to do through prayer.

It's also a way to show how much we depend on God. It teaches us to be humble and trust the Lord, not ourselves. When you pray, you're admitting there's a greater power than you out there.

Elijah understood that. He knew that on his own, he couldn't bring fire from heaven, cause it to rain, or raise the dead. But he also knew who could, so he prayed to him—and marvelous things happened.

God's heroes believe in the power of prayer!

BATTLE PLAN

Set aside 5 to 10 minutes each day to pray, and watch how God starts working mightily in your life!

A TRUE HERO FOR GOD . . . EXCITEDLY AWAITS ETERNITY IN HEAVEN.

A HERO'S TALE

Elijah's work on earth was done.

He had bravely confronted two wicked kings—Ahab and his son Ahaziah—and faithfully proclaimed God's words to wayward Israel. He had performed mighty miracles by God's power. He had anointed his successor, Elisha, to take his place as God's main prophet. And now, it was time to leave the world.

MESSAGE FROM HEADQUARTERS

WE ARE CITIZENS OF HEAVEN, WHERE THE LORD JESUS CHRIST LIVES. AND WE ARE EAGERLY WAITING FOR HIM TO RETURN AS OUR SAVIOR.
                                    – PHILIPPIANS 3:20

But Elijah wasn't going to die. God had a special plan for him. One day, Elijah and Elisha were walking near the Jordan River. Here's how the Bible describes what happened next: "As they were walking along and talking, suddenly a chariot of fire appeared, drawn by horses of fire. It drove between the two men, separating them, and Elijah was carried by a whirlwind into heaven" (2 Kings 2:11). Wow, what a way to go!

God rewarded Elijah's lifetime of faithfulness with a wonderfully unique and mysterious experience to end his time on earth. In fact, Elijah is one of only two men in the Bible whose earthly lives didn't end in death. Do you know who the other is?

It was Enoch (see Genesis 5:23-24). Great job if you knew!

DECODING THE MESSAGE

Just as Elijah learned, this earthly life is not the end of our existence. God created humans with eternal souls. Our earthly bodies die, but our souls live forever.

When we die, our souls go to one of two places: heaven or hell. Heaven is an indescribably wonderful paradise where God dwells. Hell is a horrific destination of punishment and separation from God.

Going to heaven requires faith in Jesus. John 14:6 says no one comes to God the Father except through Jesus.

Jesus Christ died on the cross to pay the penalty for your sins, and then he rose from the dead so that you could live eternally with him. If you believe this good news of God's salvation—the gospel—you can avoid being eternally separated from God and go to heaven, too, just like Elijah!

Maybe you're wondering what heaven will be like. While the Bible doesn't give us full details, the book of Revelation reveals there will be no sin or death in heaven. There won't be any sickness, sadness, or suffering, either. Best of all, we will forever enjoy perfect, face-to-face fellowship with the Lord—the way he originally intended before sin messed up everything.

Heaven can't come soon enough!

BATTLE PLAN

To learn more about heaven, read Revelation 21:1–22:5. Other good passages about life after death include 1 Corinthians 15 and 1 Thessalonians 4:13-18.

DAY 43

SHOWS KINDNESS EVEN TO ENEMIES.

A HERO'S TALE

In 2 Kings 5, the Bible tells a short but wonderful story of a little Jewish girl. Her story is so brief, the Bible doesn't even mention her name. But her heroic act of kindness has been remembered for thousands of years through Scripture.

> **MESSAGE FROM HEADQUARTERS**
>
> BLESS THOSE WHO PERSECUTE YOU. DON'T CURSE THEM; PRAY THAT GOD WILL BLESS THEM.
> – ROMANS 12:14

Life was very difficult for this girl. She lived in the ninth century BC, when Israel was at war with lots of neighboring countries like Aram, Ammon, and Moab.

During one particular raid on Israel, the Arameans plundered an Israelite town and took captives, including this girl. Naaman, the Aramean army's top general, made this girl his wife's personal servant.

Naaman was a very powerful man, but he had an awful skin disease called leprosy. The slave girl could have made fun of Naaman or remained silent and simply rejoiced in Naaman's misery. After all, he was the enemy—the leader of the army that had attacked her country and turned her world upside down.

Instead, the girl did something shocking: she encouraged Naaman to visit Elisha, Israel's mighty prophet who had miraculously healed others through God's power, so he could be cured. It was a remarkable act of kindness that probably stunned Naaman.

DECODING THE MESSAGE

Have you ever had enemies? It can seem downright impossible to get along with them. They never seem to do anything friendly to you, so it seems ridiculous to do anything kind to them.

But that's exactly what the Bible tells us to do. Take the little slave girl's example. She had every reason to hate Naaman and do everything she could to harm him. Instead, she showed him amazing kindness. She was a girl who did something big for God!

And guess what happened? Naaman put his faith in the Lord! After God healed Naaman's leprosy through Elisha, Naaman exclaimed, "Now I know that there is no God in all the world except in Israel" (2 Kings 5:15). All because a little slave girl decided to show kindness to her enemy.

God calls you to do the same. Whom can you show undeserved kindness to?

BATTLE PLAN

Make a list of the people who mistreat you. Now, write a kindness you can show them beside each of their names and make plans to do it.

GOSPEL CONNECTION

Speaking of enemies, did you know that you started out in life as God's enemy? The Bible says we are all separated from God because of our sins. But in history's greatest act of undeserved kindness, Jesus died to reconcile us (or make us right) with God. To learn more, read Colossians 1:21-23.

DAY 44

IS JOYFULLY PATIENT IN TRIALS.

A HERO'S TALE

MESSAGE FROM HEADQUARTERS

As you read yesterday, life must have been very difficult for the little Jewish slave girl in 2 Kings 5.

> BE JOYFUL IN HOPE, PATIENT IN AFFLICTION, FAITHFUL IN PRAYER.
> – ROMANS 12:12, NIV

Imagine being with your family one day, just like normal, when suddenly enemy soldiers invade your town. They loot your home, steal all your valuables, and destroy everything else. Then someone grabs you and ties you up with other captives and forces you to march to a foreign country, ripping you away from everything you've ever known.

That would be terrible, right? Well, that's what happened to this little girl. She was forced into slavery in the household of Naaman, the Aramean army's commanding general.

Where were the girl's parents? Were they also taken as prisoners? Were they killed in the raid? The Bible doesn't say. But it seems like they weren't with her, or the Bible probably would have mentioned them in 2 Kings 5:2-3. The girl must have felt terribly alone.

In the midst of this great trial, or difficulty, the girl could have questioned if God existed or if he had abandoned her. She could have become angry, impatient, or depressed. But she didn't. As we learned yesterday, she actually looked for ways to help her master, Naaman, who had leprosy. Stuck in a rotten situation, she made the most of it with a joyful heart.

DECODING THE MESSAGE

Sometimes life seems unfair. Trials are no fun. After all, who would choose difficulty over peace and happiness?

But life is full of trouble. Tough times are certain to come. The question is what your attitude will be when they do. Passages such as James 1:2-4 and 1 Peter 1:6-7 tell us that God allows trials in our lives to help us grow in godliness. Trials help us trust in God and develop good character traits like joy, hope, patience, and perseverance.

Tough times don't give us a free pass to have a bad attitude—quite the opposite. Believe it or not, the Bible says we are actually to rejoice during trouble (see James 1:2)! A true hero for God is joyfully patient in trials, trusting God without complaining or losing heart.

How is this possible? By remembering God's unchanging character. He loves you and will never leave you (see Deuteronomy 31:8; Matthew 28:20). He always looks out for your best interests (see Romans 8:28). With God on your side, you have nothing to fear (see Isaiah 41:10)!

BATTLE PLAN

The best way to maintain a godly attitude through trials is to remember God's promises in Scripture and pray. When tough times come, make sure you jump into God's Word and get on your knees!

A TRUE HERO FOR GOD . . . AVOIDS BITTERNESS TOWARD OTHERS.

A HERO'S TALE

Take a quick look at the two verses that tell the brief but powerful story of the little Jewish slave girl in 2 Kings 5:2-3.

At this time Aramean raiders had invaded the land of Israel, and among their captives was a young girl who had been given to Naaman's wife as a maid. One day the girl said to her mistress, "I wish my master would go to see the prophet in Samaria. He would heal him of his leprosy."

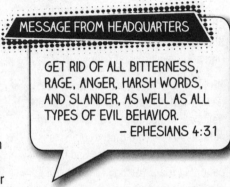

MESSAGE FROM HEADQUARTERS

GET RID OF ALL BITTERNESS, RAGE, ANGER, HARSH WORDS, AND SLANDER, AS WELL AS ALL TYPES OF EVIL BEHAVIOR.
– EPHESIANS 4:31

This little girl is one of the least-known characters in the Bible. Her whole life is summed up in exactly 56 words. We don't know her name or what Israelite town she came from. Yet those 56 words pack the spiritual punch of a heavyweight boxer.

We've talked about how this girl showed kindness to her enemies and exhibited joyful patience during a severe trial. But what about her lack of bitterness? Even though Naaman was responsible for completely ruining her former life, it seems she held no bitterness toward him. No grudge holding. No anger boiling deep down. Nothing.

And it doesn't appear she was bitter at God, either, for allowing this great difficulty to come her way. Otherwise, she would have sulked and complained rather than suggesting that Naaman visit God's prophet, Elisha, to be healed of his leprosy.

No, there was no bitterness in her. Scripture might not tell us much about this little girl, but she sure can teach us a lot!

DECODING THE MESSAGE

Spiritually speaking, bitterness can be deadly.

Bitterness is lingering anger we feel toward people when we don't forgive them. It acts like a slow-working poison, gradually killing the love, compassion, and forgiveness that God wants in our hearts. Staying angry at these people—no matter who they are or what they've done to you—is wrong. That's why today's verse commands us to "get rid of all bitterness."

We need to heed the lesson of the girl in 2 Kings 5. No matter how other people mistreat us, we are to forgive and love and to avoid bitterness at all costs.

BATTLE PLAN

Are there people who have wronged you? Go forgive them in person as soon as possible to keep bitterness from poisoning your heart.

GOSPEL CONNECTION

Jesus is the greatest example of avoiding bitterness. He had every right to be bitter at Israel's religious leaders who hated him, the Roman soldiers who crucified him, and the people who mocked his suffering. But as the perfect Son of God hung on the cross for our sins, he prayed, "Father, forgive them, for they don't know what they are doing" (Luke 23:34).

JOASH

JOASH: THE HERO WHO REPAIRED GOD'S TEMPLE

DAY 46

USES HIS SPIRITUAL GIFTS FOR GOD'S GLORY AND THE GOOD OF OTHERS.

A HERO'S TALE

Admit it: at some point, your bedroom has looked like a trash dump. Bed unmade; toys strewn across the floor; dirty clothes hanging from doorknobs; some unidentified, gooey substance sitting in the corner—not a pretty sight.

> **MESSAGE FROM HEADQUARTERS**
>
> GOD HAS GIVEN EACH OF YOU A GIFT FROM HIS GREAT VARIETY OF SPIRITUAL GIFTS. USE THEM WELL TO SERVE ONE ANOTHER.
> – 1 PETER 4:10

But even at its worst, your bedroom has nothing on how God's holy temple looked when Joash became king.

Joash (who was also called Jehoash) assumed the throne of Judah, the southern kingdom of God's people, in 835 BC after earlier wicked rulers had plunged the nation into chaos and idolatry (see 2 Kings 8–11 and 2 Chronicles 21–22).

As Baal worship grew in Judah, the people neglected God's temple. The building began showing its age, and no one bothered to clean or repair it. The sons of evil Queen Athaliah, who ruled Judah before Joash, even stole some of the temple's holy instruments and used them for Baal worship.

But all that ended when Joash became king at age seven. He was zealous about renewing the temple and personally oversaw the repairs. After many years of hard work, he "restored the Temple of God according to its original design and strengthened it" (2 Chronicles 24:13).

Nice job, Joash!

DECODING THE MESSAGE

Joash had a passion for the temple, and he possessed administrative abilities (like organization, delegation, etc.) to match. God has given you different spiritual gifts, abilities, and passions too. One of your jobs in life is to discover your gifts and use them for God's glory and the good of others.

First, let's make something clear: passions and spiritual gifts are often different from each other. You might excel at video games, but scoring high in Angry Birds or Mario Kart is not a spiritual gift! A spiritual gift is any ability that the Holy Spirit has given you to use for building up God's people, the church.

However, you *can* put your passions to good use. Joash took his passion (restoring the temple) and matched it with his spiritual gift (administration) and accomplished greatness for God.

Here's how you can learn what your spiritual gifts are:

- Read these Bible passages: Romans 12:6-8; 1 Corinthians 12:7-10, 28; Ephesians 4:11; and 1 Peter 4:10-11.
- Ask God to reveal your gifts to you.
- Ask others (like your parents) what they think your gifts might be.

What are you passionate about? Sports? Music? Art? Writing? Science? Whatever it is, match it with your spiritual gift and give God the glory!

BATTLE PLAN

Write down two lists: your passions and your spiritual gifts. Then figure out ways to combine the two, if possible.

A TRUE HERO FOR GOD . . . UNDERSTANDS THAT HIS BODY IS GOD'S NEW TEMPLE.

A HERO'S TALE

Today, the temple that King Solomon built and King Joash restored is long gone.

It was destroyed in 586 BC when King Nebuchadnezzar and the Babylonians attacked Jerusalem and took many Jews captive. Forty-seven years later, the Persian Empire conquered Babylon and allowed the Jewish exiles to return to their homeland. That's when two Jewish leaders named Zerubbabel and Joshua started building a new, much smaller temple in Jerusalem.

MESSAGE FROM HEADQUARTERS

DON'T YOU REALIZE THAT YOUR BODY IS THE TEMPLE OF THE HOLY SPIRIT, WHO LIVES IN YOU AND WAS GIVEN TO YOU BY GOD? YOU DO NOT BELONG TO YOURSELF, FOR GOD BOUGHT YOU WITH A HIGH PRICE. SO YOU MUST HONOR GOD WITH YOUR BODY.
— 1 CORINTHIANS 6:19-20

Fast-forward about 500 years to 20 BC, after the Romans had conquered much of the ancient world. At that time, King Herod (the Roman-appointed ruler of Palestine who we read about in the New Testament) renovated and greatly expanded Zerubbabel's temple. But 90 years later, when the Jews revolted against Rome in AD 70, the Romans attacked Jerusalem and destroyed Herod's temple. In the 2,000 years since then, it has never been rebuilt.

DECODING THE MESSAGE

Why the history lesson on the old Jewish temple? Because as important as that building was to ancient Israel's worship system, God never intended for his people to use a man-made building forever.

Now, *we* have become God's temple! Yep, you heard that correctly. When you put your faith in Jesus, God's Spirit comes to live inside you, making *you* God's temple, the place where his Spirit resides (see 1 Corinthians 3:16-17 and Ephesians 2:19-22). Because of this incredible truth, you can worship God anywhere because the same Spirit of God that filled Solomon's temple now fills the heart of every true Christian!

However, the Bible does say that until Jesus returns to earth again, Christians are to gather regularly with other believers (see Hebrews 10:24-25). This is what the Bible calls "the church." When God's Word talks about "the church," it's not referring to a nice building with a steeple or stained-glass windows. It's referring to all followers of Jesus around the world. If you are a Christian, you are part of "the church," and God calls you to gather frequently with other believers to grow in your faith.

But you don't have to be in a building to worship God. You can worship him anywhere, anytime, because your body is a living temple where his Holy Spirit resides. Amazing!

BATTLE PLAN

Talk to your parents about how you can worship God with your body (that is, God's temple), just like today's Scripture passage says.

DAY 48

SURROUNDS HIMSELF WITH GODLY INFLUENCES.

A HERO'S TALE

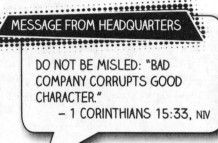

MESSAGE FROM HEADQUARTERS

DO NOT BE MISLED: "BAD COMPANY CORRUPTS GOOD CHARACTER."
– 1 CORINTHIANS 15:33, NIV

Joash started out so well.

A king by age seven, he devoted much of his life to repairing God's temple and restoring proper worship in Judah. He also listened to his mentor, the godly priest Jehoiada.

But later in life, Joash wasn't a hero at all. Like King Solomon a century earlier, his once-admirable life ended in tragedy.

By the end of his 40-year reign, Joash was worshiping false Canaanite gods and sending all the gold in the temple and palace treasuries to Syria's King Hazael to avoid a war. At age 47, Joash was murdered.

Why the terrible downfall? The answer can be found in 2 Chronicles 24:17: "After Jehoiada's death, the leaders of Judah came and bowed before King Joash and persuaded him to listen to their advice."

These "leaders" were influential politicians who didn't love the Lord. Through their wicked influence, Joash abandoned God, forgot about the very temple he had worked so hard to restore, and started bowing to false idols. Things got so bad that when a godly man named Zechariah—Jehoiada's son—criticized Joash, the king had him stoned to death within the temple grounds. He killed his mentor's son, a man he had probably grown up with!

Later that year, a small Syrian army defeated Joash's much larger force and badly wounded the king. As Joash was recovering in bed, two of his servants killed him.

It was God's judgment on Joash's wickedness.

DECODING THE MESSAGE

Joash was a good king while Jehoiada was alive. But he took a sharp turn for the worse when he started listening to ungodly influences. In short, Joash had bad friends.

What kind of friends do you have? Do they love God, or do they make fun of Christianity? Do they encourage you to obey your parents and do what's right, or do they lead you into trouble?

Choosing the right friends is really important. As today's verse says, even if you have good character, bad friends can quickly damage your life. Another great verse to consider is Proverbs 13:20, which says, "Walk with the wise and become wise; associate with fools and get in trouble."

Don't be a fool like Joash became. Surround yourself with godly friends!

BATTLE PLAN

Talk honestly to your parents about who your friends are to see if you've surrounded yourself with any bad influences. You might have to make some hard decisions and stop certain friendships. But overall, you'll be better off.

A TRUE HERO FOR GOD . . .   UNDERSTANDS GOD'S CHARACTER.

A HERO'S TALE

Have you ever played hide-and-seek?
Of course you have. Every kid has
played that game.

But imagine playing hide-and-seek with the
following rules:

1. You can only hide in the same room
   the seeker is already in.

2. The room is small, with no hiding
   places whatsoever.

3. The seeker can keep his eyes open
   the whole time you're trying to hide.

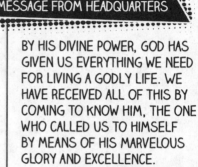

MESSAGE FROM HEADQUARTERS

BY HIS DIVINE POWER, GOD HAS
GIVEN US EVERYTHING WE NEED
FOR LIVING A GODLY LIFE. WE
HAVE RECEIVED ALL OF THIS BY
COMING TO KNOW HIM, THE ONE
WHO CALLED US TO HIMSELF
BY MEANS OF HIS MARVELOUS
GLORY AND EXCELLENCE.
– 2 PETER 1:3

Sounds like a pretty pathetic game, huh? Welcome to Jonah's world.

Jonah was a prophet in Israel who lived in the eighth century BC, when the Assyrian
Empire was the world's major superpower. The Assyrians were a wicked, violent, idol-
worshiping nation. (You can read his whole story in the short Bible book that's named
after him.)

One day, God called Jonah to travel to Nineveh, a major city in Assyria that was a 500-
mile journey northeast from Israel, and prophesy against it. But Jonah didn't want to go,
so he boarded a ship for Tarshish—the opposite direction.

You probably know the story. God sent a huge storm, the sailors threw Jonah overboard,
and a giant fish swallowed him up and spit him out on dry ground three days later. Then,
Jonah finally obeyed and went to Nineveh, where he spoke God's words to the people.

Phew, what a trip!

DECODING THE MESSAGE

Jonah was badly mistaken. He thought he could somehow run away from God, as if there are places in the world where God has no control or cannot see. But that's simply not true.

God is all-powerful. He knows and sees everything. God knows whatever we do and say—even before it happens. He sees us wherever we go. Nothing we do is a secret from him. Just like that crazy game of hide-and-seek described earlier, we can't hide from God.

Jonah learned this the hard way. But you don't have to. A true hero for God understands God's character. He reads the Bible to learn more about God. He listens in church when Scripture is taught. He asks God for more wisdom.

Although this knowledge about God doesn't save you from your sins (only faith in Jesus can do that), it will help you greatly in life. Knowing that God is holy will help you worship him. Knowing God is all-powerful will help you not to fear anything. Knowing that God knows everything will help you trust and obey him. See the connection?

So seek to understand God more. The better you know the Lord God Almighty, the better your life will be!

BATTLE PLAN

Read Psalm 139:1-12 to get a glimpse of God's all-knowing, all-seeing power and how it relates to your life.

DAY 50

BELIEVES THAT SALVATION COMES FROM THE LORD.

A HERO'S TALE

What's been the grossest experience in your life? Eating a worm? Falling in a mud puddle? Having to pick up the "presents" your dog leaves in the backyard?

> **MESSAGE FROM HEADQUARTERS**
>
> MY SALVATION COMES FROM THE LORD ALONE.
> – JONAH 2:9

Whatever it was, it's nothing compared to Jonah's worst day.

Imagine living in fish guts for three whole days. That's what happened to Jonah! After Jonah was thrown overboard from the ship to Tarshish, Jonah 1:17 says, "The LORD provided a huge fish to swallow Jonah, and Jonah was in the belly of the fish three days and three nights" (NIV). Ewwww.

How did Jonah eat, sleep, and breathe? And when he did breathe . . . oh, the stench!

We don't know exactly what those 72 hours were like for Jonah, but his runaway heart turned back toward God during that time. Inside the fish, Jonah prayed and thanked God for saving him (see Jonah 2). He acknowledged that if God hadn't sent the fish to swallow him, he certainly would have drowned.

After Jonah's three-day antipleasure cruise, the fish "vomited Jonah onto dry land" (Jonah 2:10, NIV). The poor guy needed a shower like nobody's business!

DECODING THE MESSAGE

As Jonah found out through a very wet and smelly experience, God loves to save. God desires to love and forgive us, even though we don't deserve his salvation (see Romans 3:23).

Because of our sins, we deserve God's wrath and punishment. But God sent his Son, Jesus Christ, to suffer the punishment we deserve by dying on the cross. Now, if we trust in Jesus, God promises to save us from our sins.

Praise God that he is a God of salvation!

BATTLE PLAN

The book of Psalms often mentions God's salvation. Have a contest with a friend or family member: in five minutes, see who can find the most references to God's salvation in the Psalms. (Hint: You'll need a big sheet of paper!) Afterward, read the lists to each other and marvel at God's goodness!

GOSPEL CONNECTION

In Matthew 12, Jesus mentioned Jonah during a conversation with the hypocritical religious leaders who hated him. They had asked Jesus to perform a miracle to prove that he was God's Son. Jesus refused, saying they would see only "the sign of the prophet Jonah" (verse 39). Jesus then said, "For as Jonah was in the belly of the great fish for three days and three nights, so will the Son of Man be in the heart of the earth for three days and three nights" (verse 40).

Jesus was referring to his death and resurrection. His point was this: if Jesus' resurrection from the dead didn't convince people that he was the Son of God, nothing would.

Now the question comes to you: Do *you* believe that Jesus is God's Son, who came to save you from your sins?

A TRUE HERO FOR GOD . . .   **SHOWS COMPASSION TOWARD OTHERS.**

A HERO'S TALE

Three long days after getting thrown into the sea during his ill-fated journey to Tarshish, Jonah was on dry land again. Finally.

No sooner had Jonah scrubbed himself clean of fish guts than God told him again to warn Nineveh of coming destruction if its people didn't repent of their sins. This time, Jonah obeyed.

MESSAGE FROM HEADQUARTERS

PUT ON THEN, AS GOD'S CHOSEN ONES, HOLY AND BELOVED, COMPASSIONATE HEARTS, KINDNESS, HUMILITY, MEEKNESS, AND PATIENCE.
– COLOSSIANS 3:12, ESV

Surprisingly, after hearing Jonah's message, Nineveh's king and all the people humbled themselves before God and repented. Disaster was avoided. The city was saved!

You'd think Jonah would've been thrilled by this. But he wasn't. He got mad at God. He angrily told God, "See? I knew this would happen. That's why I tried to run away in the first place." Then he even asked God to let him die.

Why was Jonah so heartless toward Nineveh? The Bible doesn't say for sure, but remember this: Nineveh was one of the most important cities in the Assyrian Empire, and Assyria was the biggest threat to Israel's safety during Jonah's lifetime. Jonah probably thought, *The more bad that happens to Nineveh (and Assyria overall), the better for Israel.*

But God rebuked Jonah for his uncaring attitude and his desire to see more than 100,000 people destroyed. God asked Jonah, "Is it right for you to be angry about this?" (Jonah 4:4). The answer was clearly no. Sadly, Jonah lacked a compassionate heart.

DECODING THE MESSAGE

Merriam-Webster's dictionary defines compassion as "sympathetic consciousness of others' distress together with a desire to alleviate it." In other words, having compassion means hurting when other people hurt and trying to help fix their problem.

God is a God of compassion. Psalm 103:13 says, "The LORD is like a father to his children, tender and compassionate to those who fear him." Yes, God is holy and just and must punish sin, but he mixes those characteristics perfectly with love, mercy, and compassion.

Aren't you glad God is compassionate? He could have left us to die in our sins (like Jonah wanted for the Ninevites). But instead he saw us wallowing in our rebellion and compassionately reached down from heaven to help us by providing a Savior—his Son, Jesus.

We should follow this example and show compassion toward others. Do you know someone who is hurting? Reach out to that person. Listen to him or her. Give help. In doing so, you'll heroically show that hurting person the compassion of God.

BATTLE PLAN

There are plenty of ways to show compassion: visit the elderly in a nursing home, send food and supplies to orphans in a developing country, serve in a soup kitchen for the homeless, etc.

A TRUE HERO FOR GOD . . . WORSHIPS GOD AS HOLY.

A HERO'S TALE

Isaiah thought he was dead. Finished. Doomed. Kaput.

The year was 740 BC, and God's people were in serious danger. The northern kingdom of Israel had already abandoned the Lord to serve the false gods of the surrounding nations. Soon, God would punish Israel by allowing the Assyrian Empire to conquer it.

> **MESSAGE FROM HEADQUARTERS**
>
> THEY WERE CALLING OUT TO EACH OTHER, "HOLY, HOLY, HOLY IS THE LORD OF HEAVEN'S ARMIES! THE WHOLE EARTH IS FILLED WITH HIS GLORY!"
> – ISAIAH 6:3

Meanwhile, the southern kingdom, Judah, was dangerously heading down a similar path. In his love and mercy, God called Isaiah in a vision to warn Judah of coming judgment.

Isaiah's vision was marvelous, yet terrifying. In it, he saw God seated on a majestic throne in heaven, his royal robe filling the entire room. Swirling above God's throne were seraphim—mysterious, angelic creatures, each with six wings and a fiery appearance. As they flew, they shouted, "Holy, holy, holy is the LORD of Heaven's Armies! The whole earth is filled with his glory!" (Isaiah 6:3). Their voices were so powerful the entire throne room trembled and filled with smoke.

Isaiah feared for his life. How could he witness God's full glory and live? But God spared Isaiah's life. He sent one of his blazing angels to assure Isaiah that his sins were forgiven.

After that amazing experience, Isaiah boldly proclaimed God's words to Judah for about 60 years. Throughout his long life, Isaiah never forgot his incredible encounter with God's holiness.

DECODING THE MESSAGE

When the Bible describes God as holy, it means he is unique and set apart. It also means he is completely pure and sinless.

God is not like us. He is eternal; we are created. He is all-powerful and all-knowing; we are limited in power and knowledge. He is perfect; we are sinful.

Because of who he is, God deserves all of our love, praise, and honor. We are to worship him and stand in awe of his holiness, like Isaiah did.

We are also to imitate God's holiness. No, we can't be perfect too. But we should strive to be like him. God says in Leviticus 11:45, "You must be holy because I am holy."

That's a tall order. But see today's Gospel Connection for how it's possible.

BATTLE PLAN

Read Isaiah 6 and Revelation 4 to compare two different visions of God's holiness (from Isaiah and the apostle John).

GOSPEL CONNECTION

God's holiness demands punishment for sin, but Jesus took our punishment on the cross. The only way we can be truly holy (without sin) before God is through faith in Jesus. Colossians 1:22 says Jesus sacrificed himself in order to "present you holy in [God's] sight, without blemish and free from accusation" (NIV). Thank you, Jesus!

A TRUE HERO FOR GOD . . .   HAS A HEART WILLING TO SERVE GOD.

A HERO'S TALE

Imagine, for a moment, that a local coach is recruiting you to play your favorite sport on his team. Excitedly, you agree. Then he tells you, "Okay, I'm going to be honest with you: people will laugh at you and even hate you for being on this team. Most of your teammates will ignore what I tell them. And you're probably going to lose most of your games."

Would you still play for that team? No way!

> ### MESSAGE FROM HEADQUARTERS
>
> I HEARD THE LORD ASKING, "WHOM SHOULD I SEND AS A MESSENGER TO THIS PEOPLE? WHO WILL GO FOR US?" I SAID, "HERE I AM. SEND ME."
> – ISAIAH 6:8

Well, that's basically what happened to Isaiah. When God called Isaiah to be his prophet to Judah, he gave him an incredibly difficult mission: Isaiah was to warn Judah that it would be destroyed if the people didn't repent of their wickedness and turn back to God. But then God told Isaiah something strange: "Harden the hearts of these people. Plug their ears and shut their eyes" (Isaiah 6:10). When Isaiah asked how long he was to preach this message, God responded, "Until their towns are empty, their houses are deserted, and the whole country is a wasteland" (Isaiah 6:11).

In other words, before Isaiah even started, God told him that his mission would ultimately fail. People would reject him and Babylon would eventually conquer Judah, but Isaiah was to keep preaching this message until the bitter end.

Not exactly a pep talk, huh? Nevertheless, here's how Isaiah responded: "Here I am. Send me" (Isaiah 6:8).

DECODING THE MESSAGE

We don't always jump up and respond enthusiastically when asked to do something difficult or unpleasant, do we? Think about your reactions to your parents when they say,

- "Please clean your room."
- "Take out the trash."
- "Go scrub the bathrooms."

Sometimes, we drag our feet, make excuses, or just plain don't obey.

But Isaiah is a great example of having a willing heart to serve God. Isaiah's task wasn't easy or even enjoyable, but he still responded with enthusiasm when God called him.

God calls all his children to serve him somehow. What is God calling you to do? It could be something as simple as obeying your parents better or being kinder to others. Or it could be something much tougher, like being a missionary.

Whatever it is, honor God by having a willing heart to serve him. Say to him, "Here I am. Send me."

BATTLE PLAN

God may reveal your mission soon. Or you may have to wait awhile. Either way, pray for a heart that's willing to serve him.

DAY 54

THANKS JESUS FOR SUFFERING IN OUR PLACE.

A HERO'S TALE

The book of Isaiah is tough to read.

As the longest of the Old Testament's prophetic books, it's filled with harsh condemnations of sin, shocking imagery of judgment, and frightening predictions of destruction and sorrow. It is God's final warning, through the prophet Isaiah, to the people of Judah to turn from their sins before he has to punish their rebellion.

As we've discussed earlier, the people didn't listen. Eventually, the powerful Babylonian Empire fully conquered Judah (by 586 BC) and exiled many of the people to distant lands.

> ### MESSAGE FROM HEADQUARTERS
>
> HE WAS PIERCED FOR OUR TRANSGRESSIONS, HE WAS CRUSHED FOR OUR INIQUITIES; THE PUNISHMENT THAT BROUGHT US PEACE WAS ON HIM, AND BY HIS WOUNDS WE ARE HEALED.
>
> – ISAIAH 53:5, NIV

Yet mixed in with all the doom and gloom of Isaiah is a message of glorious hope. God promised to restore his people and bless them with a new kingdom of peace, joy, and forgiveness. But after all their sin against God, how was this possible?

Check out Isaiah 52:13–53:12. It's one of the most beloved passages in all Scripture. In it, Isaiah predicts the coming of a "servant" who will pay for the people's guilt and sins by his own suffering. This "Suffering Servant" is compared to a lamb (see Isaiah 53:7), connecting him to the Old Testament sacrificial system, where Jewish priests sacrificed animals at the temple altar to atone, or pay for, the people's sins.

But the Suffering Servant would be a far greater sacrifice than any animal, because his atonement would be once and for all. Never again would an animal's blood need to be shed, because the Suffering Servant would shed his own perfect blood for all mankind.

He would endure unspeakable tragedy. Isaiah's prophecy says he would be "despised and rejected" (Isaiah 53:3), "acquainted with deepest grief" (53:3), considered "punished by God, stricken by him, and afflicted" (53:4, NIV), "pierced" and "crushed" (53:5), and "so disfigured he seemed hardly human" (52:14).

And he'd do this all for you.

DECODING THE MESSAGE

Do you know who the Suffering Servant is? It's Jesus Christ!

God's own Son fulfilled Isaiah's prophecy through his crucifixion on a terrible Roman cross. Jesus endured all that pain and suffering to pay for your sins and make you right with God. Three days later, he rose from the grave, proving that God had accepted his sacrifice forever.

Now, through faith in Jesus, you can receive the blessings of God's love and forgiveness (instead of his wrath and punishment). For what he did in your place, Jesus deserves all your trust, thanks, and praise!

BATTLE PLAN

Read Isaiah 52:13–53:12 and offer a prayer of thanks to Jesus for the incredible sacrifice he made to pay for your sins.

DAY 55

A TRUE HERO FOR GOD . . .

OBEYS GOD'S WORD NO MATTER WHAT.

A HERO'S TALE

King Hezekiah was at a dangerous crossroads. The fate of the entire southern kingdom rested on him.

Hezekiah became Judah's ruler in 715 BC. His father, Ahaz, was one of Judah's most wicked kings. Ahaz put up pagan altars all over Judah, sacrificed to false Canaanite gods, and locked the doors of God's temple, hoping to extinguish the worship of the Lord.

MESSAGE FROM HEADQUARTERS

YOU HAVE CHARGED US TO KEEP YOUR COMMANDMENTS CAREFULLY. OH, THAT MY ACTIONS WOULD CONSISTENTLY REFLECT YOUR DECREES!
— PSALM 119:4-5

Making matters worse, the northern kingdom, Israel, had fallen to the mighty Assyrian Empire seven years earlier, and the Assyrians had their eye on conquering Judah, too.

So Hezekiah had a choice to make. He could follow the evil ways of Israel's and Judah's previous kings. It would have been easy to do—after all, everyone else had abandoned God. Or he could go against the flow and obey God's Word, no matter what.

Heroically, he chose the latter.

Hezekiah looked into the Old Testament law (the first five books of the Bible) and shuddered at how far Judah had fallen from following God. So he promptly

- cleansed the temple of all objects of pagan worship;
- destroyed all idols throughout Judah;
- reestablished temple worship and the sacrificial systems;
- restored the practice of tithing firstfruits to God;

- reinstituted the observance of sacred festivals, including a huge, two-week Passover celebration; and
- prayerfully trusted in God for deliverance from Assyrian King Sennacherib's massive attacking army.

Judah eventually fell to the Babylonians. But not during Hezekiah's lifetime. Other than David, Hezekiah was Judah's greatest king. He faithfully obeyed God's Word, and the Lord rewarded him greatly.

DECODING THE MESSAGE

It's not always easy to obey God's Word, is it? You're probably not tempted to worship ancient Canaanite gods like Hezekiah's fellow kings were, but there are plenty of moments when following God's commands is tough.

Maybe it's when your friends want to do something wrong. Or when your parents ask you to do something you don't want to do. Or when that annoying kid at school gets on your nerves. You just want to do what you want.

But obeying the Bible is always the right way to go. After all, God himself inspired all Scripture (see 2 Timothy 3:16), so you can always trust what it says.

Choose to obey God's Word, no matter what. As Hezekiah can tell you, it's the heroic thing to do.

BATTLE PLAN

Read all of Psalm 119. It's about loving and obeying God's Word.

DAY 56

WORSHIPS GOD REGULARLY AND JOYFULLY.

A HERO'S TALE

King Hezekiah had huge challenges ahead of him.

When he took the throne of Judah, the land was in spiritual turmoil and filled with idolatry. So he went on a mission to rid the entire country of pagan worship.

MESSAGE FROM HEADQUARTERS

WORSHIP THE LORD WITH GLADNESS. COME BEFORE HIM, SINGING WITH JOY.
— PSALM 100:2

But there was another major problem: even the people who weren't idolaters had forgotten how to worship the one true God properly. So Hezekiah decided to help them, too.

With diligence and passion, Hezekiah cleansed God's temple in Jerusalem; appointed priests (those who made sacrifices for the sins of the people) and Levites (those who took care of the temple) to perform their God-given duties; and restored the sacrificial system, sacred festivals, and tithing (giving a tenth of one's income to God). It was all part of worshiping God.

Then Hezekiah invited all his subjects (and even the few remaining citizens of the fallen northern kingdom that Assyria had not taken captive) to a great Passover celebration in Jerusalem. For two weeks, the people prayed, sang praise songs, sacrificed thousands of animals, and ate delicious food—all to remember God's love and kindness toward them. It was a rockin' party!

DECODING THE MESSAGE

Hezekiah understood the importance of worshiping God. Worship is simply giving God the honor and praise he deserves. Because of who God is (holy, all-powerful, just, loving, etc.) and what he has done for us (providing salvation from sins through Jesus), he is worthy of all our worship.

So how do we worship God? We should sing and pray to him and read his Word. We should worship together regularly with other believers at church (see Hebrews 10:24-25). Hopefully, you and your family faithfully attend a church that teaches (1) that faith in Jesus is the only way to heaven, and (2) that the Bible is inspired by God and without error.

As you do these things, keep in mind that we don't impress God or earn bonus points with him when we worship. God doesn't need to feel better about himself or have others tell him how great he is, because he's already perfect!

God doesn't *need* our worship. But he *wants* our worship because he is worthy of it and because it shows our hearts are submitted to him.

So worship God regularly and joyfully, just like Hezekiah did. God deserves it all!

BATTLE PLAN

Ask your parents about starting a daily family worship time at home. It could be reading God's Word together at the breakfast table, praying and singing praise songs before bedtime, or memorizing Scripture together. Whatever you do, make sure the focus is to glorify God!

A TRUE HERO FOR GOD . . .   PRAYS IN TIMES OF TROUBLE.

A HERO'S TALE

Like a runaway bulldozer, the Assyrian Empire was plowing through every nation in its path as it conquered much of the ancient Middle East in the eighth century BC. The Assyrians had swallowed up Babylonia, Syria, and Israel, to name a few countries. Then King Sennacherib, Assyria's prideful, power-hungry ruler, set his sights on Judah (see 2 Kings 18:19-37).

The Assyrians steamrollered into the Promised Land and weakened Judah's defenses by capturing all of its fortified cities. Next stop: Jerusalem, the capital.

MESSAGE FROM HEADQUARTERS

DO NOT BE ANXIOUS ABOUT ANYTHING, BUT IN EVERY SITUATION, BY PRAYER AND PETITION, WITH THANKSGIVING, PRESENT YOUR REQUESTS TO GOD. AND THE PEACE OF GOD, WHICH TRANSCENDS ALL UNDERSTANDING, WILL GUARD YOUR HEARTS AND YOUR MINDS IN CHRIST JESUS.
          – PHILIPPIANS 4:6-7, NIV

Before attacking, Sennacherib sent three top officials to Jerusalem's main gate to offer terms of surrender. The officers delivered a message from Sennacherib himself in which the Assyrian emperor arrogantly recounted all of his previous victories, blasphemed God as just another helpless deity that would fall to him, and predicted an easy Assyrian triumph. In short, he was saying, "Surrender or die."

It was hard to argue. No one had been able to stop Sennacherib yet. And the sight of nearly 200,000 Assyrian troops surrounding Jerusalem was enough to make the bravest warrior's knees knock. It looked like King Hezekiah and Judah were doomed.

In the face of great danger, Hezekiah responded as powerfully as he could: he prayed. Hezekiah rushed to God's temple and pleaded for God to intervene.

God's answer came quickly, miraculously, and powerfully. Before the Assyrian army could shoot a single arrow at Jerusalem, the Lord sent an angel who slaughtered 185,000 Assyrians. Sennacherib was forced to flee back to Nineveh, where he was eventually killed by two of his sons.

DECODING THE MESSAGE

Confronted by overwhelming odds, Hezekiah showed great faith in God and the power of prayer. Not many people would have responded that way. Even today, the world says that real heroes fight their own way through problems and dangers. You see it all the time in books, movies, TV shows, video games: "Don't ask for help . . . just grit your teeth, clench your fists, and battle your way out."

But that's not what the Bible teaches us to do. According to God's Word, true heroes pray on all occasions, including difficult ones.

When trouble comes, don't worry or try to fix it on your own. Just cry out to the God who can do all things. He promises to answer in the way that's best for you.

BATTLE PLAN

Memorize today's verse. It's a fantastic reminder of how to prayerfully respond to trouble.

DAY 58

AVOIDS BITTERNESS AT GOD DURING TRIALS.

A HERO'S TALE

Talk about an awful childhood.

Josiah, a king of Judah in the seventh century BC, grew up during one of the worst periods in Judah's history. All the reforms of good King Hezekiah, Josiah's great-grandfather, had been forgotten. The two kings that followed Hezekiah—Manasseh and Amon (Josiah's grandfather and father)—did more evil than any of the kings before them, according to 2 Kings 21. Two years into Amon's reign, his servants assassinated him, forcing little Josiah to become king at age eight.

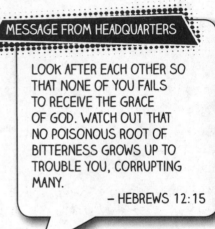

MESSAGE FROM HEADQUARTERS

LOOK AFTER EACH OTHER SO THAT NONE OF YOU FAILS TO RECEIVE THE GRACE OF GOD. WATCH OUT THAT NO POISONOUS ROOT OF BITTERNESS GROWS UP TO TROUBLE YOU, CORRUPTING MANY.

– HEBREWS 12:15

Imagine trying to lead a wicked nation of people while powerful enemies like Babylon, Egypt, and Assyria threaten you—all while you're in third grade. That's what Josiah had to do!

With his father dead, his people stuck in idolatry, and his country in serious danger, Josiah could've chosen to blame God. He could've let bitterness take root in his heart like a choking weed. He could've angrily asked God, "Why me?"

But he didn't. Instead, Josiah loved God wholeheartedly: "He did what was pleasing in the LORD's sight and followed the example of his ancestor David. He did not turn away from doing what was right" (2 Kings 22:2).

DECODING THE MESSAGE

In the chapter about the Jewish slave girl who helped Naaman, we talked about the importance of not becoming bitter toward others. But it's just as important to avoid growing bitter at God.

When life doesn't go our way, it's easy to start complaining or even blaming God for our trials. But bitterness is a dangerous sin. Hebrews 12:15 describes it as a "poisonous root" that "grows up to trouble you, corrupting many."

If we water and feed the root of bitterness, it will develop into anger and many harmful thoughts toward God and others around us.

Evil in your life is not God's fault. Rather, it's the product of the fallen, sinful world we live in. Yes, God allows us to go through difficult times, even tragedies. But this is never meant for our ultimate harm. God only wants to test our faith and draw us closer to him.

God is good. He doesn't seek to hurt us in any way. He eventually works everything— *everything!*—for the good of his children (see Romans 8:28).

A true hero for God responds to life's challenges not with bitterness, but with a deeper trust in God. Just like young Josiah.

BATTLE PLAN

Do research online or at the library on how plants grow. Use that to better understand the Bible's analogy in today's verse of bitterness being like a poisonous root.

DAY 59

A HERO'S TALE

Imagine being at the breakfast table with your family one morning. As you're wolfing down a bowl of Cap'n Crunch, someone tells you some bad news. Suddenly, you stand up, rip your clothes in half, and begin weeping loudly.

> **MESSAGE FROM HEADQUARTERS**
>
> [THE LORD SAID,] "I WILL BLESS THOSE WHO HAVE HUMBLE AND CONTRITE HEARTS, WHO TREMBLE AT MY WORD."
> – ISAIAH 66:2

Your family would probably stare at you, speechless, thinking you're cuckoo. These days, people just don't react like that.

But that's exactly what King Josiah of Judah did when his servants read him part of the Old Testament that they had discovered in the temple. In ancient times, it was customary to tear one's clothes to outwardly express extreme grief.

Why was Josiah sad? Because that portion of Scripture—which apparently had been lost or hidden during the idolatrous reigns of his father and grandfather, Amon and Manasseh—spoke of terrible judgment for the people if they worshiped other gods. (Check out the full story in 2 Kings 22 and 2 Chronicles 34.)

Because of the people's wickedness, God was going to allow the Babylonians to destroy Judah. Not even a great king like Josiah could save the nation now. But God promised that Josiah wouldn't experience Judah's downfall. Why? Because Josiah was "sorry and humbled [himself] before the LORD" (2 Kings 22:19).

DECODING THE MESSAGE

Humility is the opposite of pride and arrogance. Humility is not thinking too highly of yourself. Humility is also present when we submit ourselves to God.

This is exactly what Josiah did when he heard God's Word. He realized that there was a holy, almighty God in heaven whose love, mercy, and grace he didn't deserve. The proper response was humble repentance and prayer, and that's just what Josiah did.

In today's verse, God says very plainly that he blesses the humble. And during Jesus' earthly ministry, he told people, "Those who exalt themselves will be humbled, and those who humble themselves will be exalted" (Matthew 23:12).

The message is clear: be humble before the Lord. Give your life to him. Acknowledge that he is God and you are not. Ask him to forgive your sins and help you live righteously.

But whatever you do, please don't rip your clothes.

BATTLE PLAN

Putting others first is a great way to practice humility. Go out of your way to do something kind for someone else today.

GOSPEL CONNECTION

Jesus is the greatest example of humility ever. Read Philippians 2:1-11 to see how Jesus humbled himself for our benefit and how we should respond.

DAY 60

CHERISHES GOD'S WORD.

A HERO'S TALE

Imagine, for a moment, what would happen if the president of the United States took the stage outside the US Capitol in Washington, DC, and read aloud from the book of Deuteronomy to a crowd that included the nation's senators, representatives, Supreme Court justices, every DC resident, and many other Americans from around the country—and called everyone to obey God's laws. What a historic event that would be!

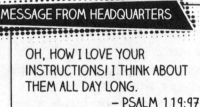

MESSAGE FROM HEADQUARTERS

OH, HOW I LOVE YOUR INSTRUCTIONS! I THINK ABOUT THEM ALL DAY LONG.

– PSALM 119:97

Well, that's basically what King Josiah did in 622 BC.

After his servants discovered the Book of the Law (probably a scroll of Deuteronomy) while repairing the temple, Josiah publicly read it at the temple, the most important building in Jerusalem, Judah's capital. In his audience were Judah's government officials, priests, prophets, all of Jerusalem's residents, and others from around the nation.

According to 2 Kings 23:3, Josiah "renewed the covenant in the LORD's presence. He pledged to obey the LORD by keeping all his commands, laws, and decrees with all his heart and soul," just like Deuteronomy 31:11 commands. After seeing Josiah's example, all the people did the same.

DECODING THE MESSAGE

Josiah cherished God's Word. To *cherish* something means to hold it dear or show affection for it. As soon as the forgotten parts of Scripture were found, Josiah cherished and obeyed them with all his heart.

What do you cherish most? A certain toy? Your PlayStation, Xbox, or Wii? Clothes? Money? Friends? It's fine to enjoy all those things, but you should cherish God's Word the most.

To do this, you've got to obey what it says. And to obey what it says, you've got to know what it says. And to know what it says, you've got to read it often. See the progression?

If you're wondering why we should cherish God's Word, the answer is simple: because it's exactly what it claims to be—the very words of the Lord God Almighty (see 2 Timothy 3:16; 2 Peter 1:20-21). The Bible—all 66 books, from Genesis to Revelation—is our guidebook for life. The Creator and Ruler of the universe has graciously provided us with an instruction manual on how to live, so we should follow it wholeheartedly.

The Bible also wonderfully details God's salvation plan for sinful humanity. It's a 100 percent–true story of how he saw our need for a Savior and answered with his Son, Jesus.

The reasons go on and on. But here's the point: cherish God's Word. You'll be glad you did.

BATTLE PLAN

Commit to reading the Bible every day. Those who cherish God's Word read it often.

JEREMIAH: THE PROPHET-HERO
WHO HAD A TOUGH JOB, PART 2

DAY 61

BELIEVES GOD'S POWER TRUMPS AGE.

A HERO'S TALE

From the list below, what's the worst thing you could hear?

1. "Don't forget—you have a dentist appointment tomorrow."

2. "You're grounded from playing video games for a week."

3. "Surprise, kids—we're having lima beans for dinner tonight!"

4. "Sorry, you're not old enough."

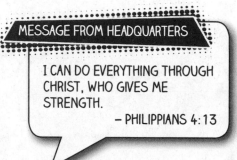

MESSAGE FROM HEADQUARTERS

I CAN DO EVERYTHING THROUGH CHRIST, WHO GIVES ME STRENGTH.

– PHILIPPIANS 4:13

If you chose number 4, today's devotional is especially for you! You're about to see how it's okay to be a kid.

In 627 BC, Josiah, Judah's last good king, was on the throne, but the nation was heading down the same path of idolatry and wickedness that had doomed the northern kingdom of Israel a century earlier. So God called a young man named Jeremiah to speak his words to the people. (Check out the story in Jeremiah 1.)

Jeremiah initially wasn't thrilled at the idea. He said, "O Sovereign LORD, . . . I can't speak for you! I'm too young!" (Jeremiah 1:6).

But God wasn't interested in excuses. So he corrected Jeremiah: "Don't say, 'I'm too young,' for you must go wherever I send you and say whatever I tell you. And don't be afraid of the people, for I will be with you and will protect you" (Jeremiah 1:7-8).

Then God did something interesting: he touched Jeremiah's mouth and assured him, "Look, I have put my words in your mouth! Today I appoint you to stand up against nations and kingdoms. Some you must uproot and tear down, destroy and overthrow. Others you must build up and plant" (Jeremiah 1:9-10).

From then on, Jeremiah fulfilled his calling. It wasn't always easy, but he prophesied powerfully for 40 years, and the book he wrote is one of the greatest in the Old Testament. All of his prophecies came true, and at least five New Testament passages quote his writings.

DECODING THE MESSAGE

Jeremiah quickly learned that age isn't a valid excuse with God. When it comes to being a godly hero, it's not about your age; it's about God's power. God created and rules the entire universe—certainly he can supply you with strength to serve him, no matter your age!

Just like God touched Jeremiah's mouth with the words to speak to Judah, he will give you the power to serve him in whatever he has called you to.

So trust in God's power. He wants to use you in mighty ways!

BATTLE PLAN

Memorize today's verse. It's short, sweet, and perfectly to the point!

A TRUE HERO FOR GOD . . . | TRUSTS IN GOD AS HIS PROTECTOR.

A HERO'S TALE

Jeremiah had a rough life. And that's putting it mildly.

For 40 years, he spoke against his own wicked countrymen in Judah, predicting the nation's doom if they didn't repent. You can imagine how much they enjoyed listening to him.

> ### MESSAGE FROM HEADQUARTERS
>
> IN TIMES OF TROUBLE, MAY THE LORD ANSWER YOUR CRY. MAY THE NAME OF THE GOD OF JACOB KEEP YOU SAFE FROM ALL HARM.
>
> – PSALM 20:1

Over the course of Jeremiah's prophetic ministry, God often asked him to do incredibly difficult things, like telling the king of Judah to his face that a Babylonian army would soon conquer him (see Jeremiah 37:17), or loudly condemning the people's sins while standing at a temple entry gate, where everyone could hear him (see 19:14-15).

Jeremiah's life was endangered on many occasions. He was accused of being a traitor, beaten multiple times, put in stocks, imprisoned, threatened with death at least twice, and even thrown into a muddy cistern, where he sank into the slime.

Talk about a difficult life! It got so bad that there were times when Jeremiah wished he hadn't even been born (see Jeremiah 20:14-18).

But through it all, God remained Jeremiah's great Protector. Before Jeremiah started his ministry, God told him, "Today I have made you strong like a fortified city that cannot be captured, like an iron pillar or a bronze wall. You will stand against the whole land—the kings, officials, priests, and people of Judah. They will fight you, but they will fail. For I am with you, and I will take care of you" (Jeremiah 1:18-19).

Jeremiah's enemies never prevailed against him. God kept his promise to the very end.

DECODING THE MESSAGE

Trouble will come to you in this life. That's a guarantee. (Hopefully not as bad as Jeremiah experienced, though!) The question is, what are you going to do when trouble comes? Will you fear and lose faith? Will you rely on your own strength? Or will you trust in God as your great Protector?

A true hero doesn't try to solve life's problems on his own. He trusts in a power greater than himself.

God is faithful. He won't leave you. He loves his children and will be with you regardless of the trouble that comes your way. So trust in him!

BATTLE PLAN

One of the best ways to trust in God's protection is to pray. Whenever you're in trouble, cry out to the God who loves and protects you!

DAY 63

A HERO'S TALE

Early in Jeremiah's ministry, God told him to do something interesting. He wanted Jeremiah to travel into what was formerly the northern kingdom of Israel and give the people an important message.

Assyria had conquered Israel 100 years earlier. The people living in Israel during Jeremiah's life were a mixed race of Israelites and different pagan ethnic groups that Assyria had resettled there. The people had intermarried and combined their reli-gions, trying to worship both the one true God and many false idols. Bad idea.

MESSAGE FROM HEADQUARTERS

"THE TIME PROMISED BY GOD HAS COME AT LAST!" [JOHN THE BAPTIST] ANNOUNCED. "THE KINGDOM OF GOD IS NEAR! REPENT OF YOUR SINS AND BELIEVE THE GOOD NEWS!"
— MARK 1:15

So Jeremiah spoke God's words to the people: "O Israel, my faithless people, come home to me again, for I am merciful. I will not be angry with you forever. Only acknowl-edge your guilt. Admit that you rebelled against the LORD your God and . . . refused to listen to my voice" (Jeremiah 3:12-13).

Despite Israel's wickedness, God mercifully offered his people a second chance. But Israel had to do something to receive his forgiveness. Can you guess what it was? (Hint: Look again at the verses above and find the command God gave them.)

DECODING THE MESSAGE

Did you make your guess? Good. Here's the answer: God told the people they must "acknowledge [their] guilt." (Great job if you got the answer right!) In other words, God wanted them to repent.

To understand how we can be saved from our sins, we have to understand repentance. First, we must understand that it is God's grace, not our own efforts, that saves us. If God didn't call people to himself, no one would be saved.

But we have a responsibility too. When God's Spirit pulls on our hearts, we must respond. That response, as Jeremiah 3:13 and today's verse say, is to repent. Repenting involves several things:

- feeling godly sorrow for our sin
- turning from sin
- making a commitment to follow Jesus

Repenting is not just saying "I'm sorry." It involves a heart that truly wants to stop sinning and obey God. It's doing a 180-degree turn from a life of sin and choosing a life of faith and obedience to God instead.

So spin the wheel on sin, repent, and turn to God!

BATTLE PLAN

Have you disobeyed God recently? Practice repentance by praying the following: "God, I'm sorry for _____ [name your sin]. Please forgive me and help me to obey you instead."

GOSPEL CONNECTION

Today's verse tells us to repent of our sins *and* believe the Good News. The Good News is the gospel—the truth that Jesus died for our sins and rose from the dead. So being saved from sin involves repenting (turning from sin) and believing (trusting in Jesus).

A TRUE HERO FOR GOD . . . AVOIDS WORLDLY DEFILEMENT.

A HERO'S TALE

Daniel took one look at the dinner plate before him, frowned, and said, "No, thanks."

If it had been a tall pile of liver and onions, salty sardines, or steaming spinach—well then, yeah, who *wouldn't* push that away? But the food set before Daniel was from the king's own delicious gourmet menu! Still, Daniel politely declined.

> **MESSAGE FROM HEADQUARTERS**
>
> DO NOT LOVE THIS WORLD NOR THE THINGS IT OFFERS YOU, FOR WHEN YOU LOVE THE WORLD, YOU DO NOT HAVE THE LOVE OF THE FATHER IN YOU.
> – 1 JOHN 2:15

The year was 605 BC. The Babylonians, who had conquered Assyria, were now the world's greatest empire. King Nebuchadnezzar had started a series of attacks on Judah that would end with Jerusalem's destruction in 586 BC. Meanwhile, he took many Jews as captives back to Babylon. Daniel was one of them.

But when Daniel arrived in Babylon, he was treated like a prince, not a prisoner. The Babylonians offered him the best food and education possible. Only Daniel didn't want to eat from the king's table.

Perhaps he was trying to follow the Jewish dietary laws found in Leviticus 11 and Deuteronomy 14. It's also possible that the king's food and drink had been dedicated to idols. Whatever the reason, the Bible says that Daniel "was determined not to defile himself by eating the food and wine given to [him] by the king" (Daniel 1:8). Instead, he asked for veggies and water, and God blessed him by keeping him healthy and strong (see 1:11-15).

DECODING THE MESSAGE

The word *defile* means "to make unclean or impure." By not eating Babylonian meat, Daniel took an impressive stand for righteousness even though he was technically a prisoner of war. He wanted to keep his unique identity as a follower of the one true God of Israel rather than become like the pagan idol worshipers all around him.

Today, God calls us to avoid worldly defilement too. So what defiles you? Is it certain food? No! In Mark 7:15, Jesus said, "It's not what goes into your body that defiles you; you are defiled by what comes from your heart."

We are defiled by the sin in our hearts—pride, selfishness, greed, jealousy, lies, hatred, and so on. That's why we need God's forgiveness, which is exactly what Jesus offers us through his death on the cross!

Once we receive God's forgiveness through faith in Jesus, we must strive to be godly. God calls us to be different from the world around us. We are to obey God and avoid defiling ourselves with sinful, worldly pursuits. Sound hard—maybe even impossible? Thankfully, we have access to God's limitless power! He will help us obey him when we ask.

Put your faith in Jesus, follow God's Word, and be different from the evil world around you. Then, just like Daniel, you'll be a true hero for God!

BATTLE PLAN

To understand more about what defiles us and what doesn't, read Mark 7.

GOSPEL CONNECTION

Jesus is the perfect example of avoiding worldly defilement. He never sinned—not even once! He resisted specific attacks from the devil (see Matthew 4) and all other temptations to sin (see 2 Corinthians 5:21; Hebrews 4:15). Because Jesus had no sin, he is the only person who can take away *our* sins!

DAY 65

OBEYS GOD DESPITE ANY THREAT OF PERSECUTION.

A HERO'S TALE

This is a story about a senior citizen, ravenous lions, and faithful prayer.

By Daniel 6—the famous story of Daniel and the lions' den—Daniel was an old man. The Persian Empire was now ruling the ancient Middle East, and Daniel was probably in his 80s at this point.

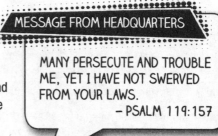

MESSAGE FROM HEADQUARTERS

MANY PERSECUTE AND TROUBLE ME, YET I HAVE NOT SWERVED FROM YOUR LAWS.
– PSALM 119:157

Daniel had lived faithfully for God in a foreign, pagan country, and God had blessed him. He was already one of King Darius's top three government officials, and he was about to get promoted. But his fellow governors were jealous and tricked Darius into making a ridiculous law: if people prayed to anyone but Darius during the next month, they would be lion food.

It was clearly a trap. The conspirators knew that Daniel prayed to God three times every day. But when he heard the new law, Daniel returned to his bedroom; opened the western window toward Jerusalem; bent down on his old, creaky knees; and prayed to God, just like always.

You can almost imagine the governors' villainous smiles. Excitedly, the evil men threw Daniel into the lions' den, but God protected him from harm because he was "innocent" (Daniel 6:22). Realizing he had been tricked, King Darius lifted Daniel out of the den the next morning and tossed in the wicked governors and their families instead. The hungry lions had a big breakfast that day. Yikes!

DECODING THE MESSAGE

Daniel continued to obey God even though he knew persecution might come. The word *persecute* means "to cause to suffer because of belief." In other words, it's when people treat others unkindly because of their faith.

It's no fun to be persecuted. Sometimes persecution involves teasing or ignoring someone. In some parts of the world, Christians are even killed for their faith. But the Bible says that Christians should expect persecution. Jesus himself said, "Since they persecuted me, naturally they will persecute you" (John 15:20).

A true hero still loves and obeys God, no matter what people do to him. After all, Jesus also said, "God blesses those who are persecuted for doing right, for the Kingdom of Heaven is theirs" (Matthew 5:10).

Fortunately, it's extremely unlikely that you'll be thrown to hungry lions for your faith (phew!). But persecution will come in some form. Stay strong in your faith. Continue to trust and obey God, and he will strengthen and bless you!

BATTLE PLAN

Ask your parents to read to you from *Foxe's Book of Martyrs*, a famous historical collection of stories about Christians who died for their faith. For other tales of current persecution, check out the Voice of the Martyrs website at www.persecution.com (with your parents' permission, of course!).

DAY 66

BELIEVES THAT GOD RULES THE WHOLE WORLD.

A HERO'S TALE

MESSAGE FROM HEADQUARTERS

Beads of sweat trickled down Daniel's forehead. His sleeping body tensed and twitched as a cool Middle Eastern breeze swept through his open bedroom window in Babylon. He was having a bad dream.

> HOW GREAT YOU ARE, O SOVEREIGN LORD! THERE IS NO ONE LIKE YOU. WE HAVE NEVER EVEN HEARD OF ANOTHER GOD LIKE YOU!
> – 2 SAMUEL 7:22

In his nighttime vision (see Daniel 7), four frightening beasts emerged from the storm-tossed waters of the Mediterranean Sea. These four beasts—a lion with eagles' wings, a bear, a leopard with bird wings, and a "terrifying" beast (7:7) with iron teeth and 10 horns—climbed ashore and destroyed everything in their paths.

Daniel's dream was a special vision of the future from God. The four beasts represented four great empires that came to power during or after Daniel's lifetime—Babylon (lion), Medo-Persia (bear), Greece (leopard), and Rome ("terrifying" beast).

God gave Daniel many other prophetic visions in his lifetime. In fact, chapters 7–12 of the book of Daniel are filled with futuristic visions.

Much of Daniel's visions predicted what would happen in the next 400 to 500 years in the ancient world. But some of Daniel's visions seem to have double meanings, also predicting events that we are still waiting to see today. And God even gave Daniel a sneak peek at the first coming of Jesus, the "son of man" (Daniel 7:13), which was still more than 500 years away from Daniel's lifetime. Amazing!

Don't feel bad if you read Daniel and come away a little confused. It's a hard book to understand, even for full-time Bible scholars!

DECODING THE MESSAGE

God didn't give Daniel these amazing glimpses into the future simply for an advance history lesson about ancient Greece or Rome. God did it to show his complete sovereignty.

The word *sovereignty* means "supreme power." God has all power in the universe. He created and rules everything. He doesn't answer to anyone. Even the mightiest kings and empires are under his control.

This must have been a great comfort to Daniel and his fellow Jews, who were scattered all over the world after the fall of Israel and Judah. Life was difficult and scary during Daniel's lifetime. Wars were everywhere. Empires rose and fell with alarming speed.

So God gave Daniel special knowledge of future events before they happened to prove that he ruled it all. He also assured Daniel that he would take care of his people.

This is an important lesson for us to learn today. God rules everything. No matter what's going on in your life or in the world around you, he is in control and he loves you!

BATTLE PLAN

Read the entire book of Daniel to learn more about this incredible hero and the all-powerful, sovereign God he served! Isaiah 40 is also a good chapter about God's sovereignty.

A TRUE HERO FOR GOD . . .   **SACRIFICES PERSONAL INTERESTS FOR THE GOOD OF OTHERS.**

A HERO'S TALE

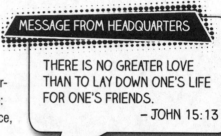

MESSAGE FROM HEADQUARTERS

THERE IS NO GREATER LOVE THAN TO LAY DOWN ONE'S LIFE FOR ONE'S FRIENDS.
– JOHN 15:13

Of all the 66 books in the Bible, Esther might be most ready made for a Hollywood movie script. It has all the important ingredients for a major motion picture: heroes, a villain, danger, suspense, romance, irony, comedy, poetic justice, and a happy ending.

Esther lived in the mid-fifth century BC, when the Persian Empire was at the height of its power. She was a beautiful Jewish girl who was an exile in the Persian capital of Susa. By God's will, she became King Xerxes's queen and discovered a terrible plot by a wicked man named Haman to kill all the Jews in Persia.

There was only one thing for Esther to do: approach Xerxes and plead for the lives of her fellow Jews. But it wasn't that simple. In ancient Persia, you couldn't just stroll into the king's throne room and ask a favor. If you displeased the king at all (even as his queen), you could be executed. Yikes!

It was a terribly risky move. But Esther knew what she had to do for the good of her people, even if it meant her own death. So she made up her mind: "Though it is against the law, I will go in to see the king. If I must die, I must die" (Esther 4:16).

But God protected Esther. Xerxes showed favor to her, Haman was executed, and the Jews were saved!

DECODING THE MESSAGE

Esther was a true hero for God because she was willing to sacrifice her own life for the good of others. The Bible calls this the ultimate expression of love (see today's verse).

Now, don't get confused. You don't have to die for others to show them love. But you do need to put others' needs before your own. It's all part of being humble and considering others better than yourself, as Philippians 2 says.

BATTLE PLAN

Read the Gospel Connection on this page and then spend a few minutes thanking Jesus for sacrificing himself for your good.

GOSPEL CONNECTION

When it comes to sacrificing yourself for the good of others, no one in history did it better than Jesus. God's Son gave up heaven's glory to be born as a human baby in a wicked world. Despite his sinless life, he endured ridicule, rejection, abandonment, unspeakable torture, and finally death on a vicious Roman cross—all so that sinners like us could be made right with a holy God. *That* is true sacrifice!

A TRUE HERO FOR GOD . . . GLORIFIES THE LORD IN THE MIDST OF UNBELIEVERS.

A HERO'S TALE

Esther might have been a queen, but life was certainly not easy for her.

Although she was Jewish, Esther lived far away from Israel. The Assyrians and Babylonians had conquered her people many years earlier. Her parents had died while she was still young (see Esther 2:7), so Mordecai, her older cousin, had raised her.

MESSAGE FROM HEADQUARTERS

LET YOUR LIGHT SHINE BEFORE OTHERS, THAT THEY MAY SEE YOUR GOOD DEEDS AND GLORIFY YOUR FATHER IN HEAVEN.

– MATTHEW 5:16, NIV

Esther lived in Susa, the capital of the Persian Empire, which was hundreds of miles from her ancestral home in Israel. The people of Persia didn't believe in the one true God. Some Persians followed a false religion called Zoroastrianism, which taught about a supreme god but didn't have much else in common with the truth of the Bible. Others in the empire were polytheistic, meaning they worshiped many false gods.

It would have been easy for Esther to go with the flow in Susa. Acting like everyone else would've been the safest thing to do. To be different meant potentially being ridiculed, excluded, or even killed.

But Esther chose to glorify God by standing up for what was right and saving God's people from being destroyed.

Go, Esther!

DECODING THE MESSAGE

It's easy to follow God when you're around Christians, isn't it? But what about when no other believers are around?

Just like Esther, you probably know plenty of people who don't believe in the Bible or follow God. Perhaps they're kids at school or in your neighborhood or maybe even family members.

They might use bad language or think it's okay to lie or constantly disobey or disrespect their parents. Maybe they steal, cheat, or think going to church is a waste of time.

It's not easy to act differently around them, is it? But being different from the world is what being a godly hero is all about. God wants us to glorify him, no matter who's around. And that means obeying him around unbelievers as well as Christians.

The Bible calls this "shining your light" (see today's verse). The world is a dark place because of sin. By being different and glorifying God around unbelievers, you can shine the light (and love) of God into sin's darkness.

So turn on that God-powered light and shine, baby, shine!

BATTLE PLAN

Memorize today's verse. It's a great reminder for when you're surrounded by unbelievers like Esther was in Susa.

DAY 69

CELEBRATES GOD'S GOODNESS.

A HERO'S TALE

MESSAGE FROM HEADQUARTERS

The threat was over. Wicked Haman—and everyone else throughout Persia who wanted to destroy the Jews—had been executed. Esther and Mordecai were heroes. God's people were saved.

> I WILL REMEMBER THE DEEDS OF THE LORD; YES, I WILL REMEMBER YOUR MIRACLES OF LONG AGO.
> – PSALM 77:11, NIV

Now, it was time to party!

Mordecai, whom King Xerxes promoted to his second-in-command, and Esther sent letters to Jews everywhere in the vast Persian Empire, telling them to celebrate Purim. This new, two-day holiday was all about remembering God's deliverance of his people. Esther 9:22 says that Jews were to celebrate Purim "with feasting and gladness and by giving gifts of food to each other and presents to the poor."

Today, almost 2,500 years later, Jews still celebrate Purim, usually each March. During the holiday, Jews often read the entire book of Esther, and the listeners boo, hiss, stomp their feet, or shake noisemakers whenever Haman's name is mentioned. It's also customary during Purim to send gifts of food and drink to others and give money to charities.

Some Jews host carnival-like celebrations on Purim, performing plays and holding beauty contests. Other Purim traditions include greeting others with a phrase such as "*Chag Purim Sameach*!" ("Happy Purim Holiday!" for those of you who don't speak Hebrew), masquerading, singing Purim songs, and eating yummy pastries called "Haman's ears" and "Haman's pockets."

DECODING THE MESSAGE

Esther and Mordecai thought it was important to remember God's deliverance. So they wrote, "This Festival of Purim would never cease to be celebrated among the Jews" (Esther 9:28).

Purim is one of many holy festivals the ancient Jews celebrated, including the weekly Sabbath and the annual feasts of Passover, Firstfruits, Weeks, Trumpets, Booths, and the Day of Atonement. All these special events remembered different aspects of God's goodness toward Israel.

It's important for us to remember God's goodness too. What do you do to celebrate this? Do you read his Word to learn about all he's done for you? Do you thank him through prayer? Do you worship him through songs and music? Do you tell others about the good things he's given you? All of this is important to do.

As humans, we tend to forget things quickly. But the Bible is full of commands to remember all the blessings God has given us. God's greatest gift to us is that he sent his own Son, Jesus, to die for our sins.

God has been so kind and loving to you. Celebrate his goodness!

BATTLE PLAN

Have you put your faith in Jesus? If so, plan a "Celebrating God's Goodness" party on the date you were saved. Ask your parents for help to plan fun activities and turn it into an annual celebration of God's goodness to you!

DAY 70

TRUSTS IN GOD FOR WHAT SEEMS IMPOSSIBLE.

A HERO'S TALE

Heaven had been silent a long time.

It had been about 450 years since God had spoken to his people through the prophets. The Romans now ruled most of the ancient world, and God's people, the Jews, were spread out all over the empire. It was a scary, confusing time.

> ### MESSAGE FROM HEADQUARTERS
>
> JESUS LOOKED AT THEM AND SAID, "WITH MAN THIS IS IMPOSSIBLE, BUT WITH GOD ALL THINGS ARE POSSIBLE."
> — MATTHEW 19:26, NIV

All the while, God's people were waiting for the Messiah, or Savior, that Scripture had promised. But where was he? When would he come? Had God forgotten them? The people waited . . . and waited . . . and waited.

And then one day in the small town of Nazareth, the angel Gabriel visited a young Jewish woman named Mary and delivered a shocking message: soon, she would give birth to the Savior, God's own Son.

Mary wasn't married, so she asked the angel, "How will this be?" Gabriel answered, "The Holy Spirit will come upon you, and the power of the Most High will overshadow you. So the baby to be born will be holy, and he will be called the Son of God" (Luke 1:35).

Mary was scared and puzzled. But she responded, "I am the Lord's servant. May everything you have said about me come true" (Luke 1:38). The birth of Jesus would be a mind-blowing miracle. But Mary answered this incredible promise with incredible faith!

DECODING THE MESSAGE

Imagine if an angel suddenly appeared to you and promised you'd be able to fly. Or breathe underwater like a fish. Or shoot lightning bolts from your fingertips.

Would you believe him?

What Gabriel told Mary sounded just as crazy. In fact, it was humanly impossible. Mary had no idea how it would happen. And yet she believed God anyway. That's true faith—believing without seeing (see Hebrews 11:1).

We're called to show the same faith in God. Why? Because God can do the impossible. There's no limit to his power or abilities. He created the universe, so he can do anything in his universe that pleases him.

God is a big God, and our faith in him needs to be big too. Whatever your situation is, God can do what seems impossible, like today's verse says. You might not know how he's going to do it, but you can trust that God—in his goodness, wisdom, and love—will work mightily on your behalf.

BATTLE PLAN

List all of God's miracles you can think of from the Bible. (Hint: You might need several pieces of paper!) This should build your faith to trust in the God who can do the impossible!

A TRUE HERO FOR GOD . . . | PRAISES GOD FOR HIS GLORIOUS DEEDS.

A HERO'S TALE

Mary—a young, unimportant woman from a small, unimportant town in Israel—had just received some astonishing news. God was going to use her in his greatest miracle since the creation of the world—greater than Noah's flood or the 10 plagues in Egypt or the parting of the Red Sea.

Mary was going to give birth to the Son of God.

> **MESSAGE FROM HEADQUARTERS**
>
> MARY RESPONDED, "OH, HOW MY SOUL PRAISES THE LORD. HOW MY SPIRIT REJOICES IN GOD MY SAVIOR!"
>
> – LUKE 1:46-47

She could have reacted in many ways. But she chose to respond in faith and praise toward God. After learning that her relative Elizabeth had a miraculous baby (John the Baptist) growing inside of her, too, Mary wrote one of the Bible's most beautiful songs of praise. It later became known as "the Magnificat" (a Latin word meaning "magnifies" or "glorifies"). You can read it in Luke 1:46-55.

In the Magnificat, Mary bubbled over with excitement about the Lord's glorious characteristics (such as his power, holiness, and strength) and his wonderful deeds (how he cares for his children, keeps his promises, and acts as our Savior). She also marveled at how God humbles the proud but exalts the humble (like her).

Mary's Magnificat might not have made any top-40 music charts in first-century Palestine, but it's still an awesome song!

DECODING THE MESSAGE

When God blessed Mary, she praised him from the depths of her soul. What's your response to God's kindness and love toward you? Do you offer God a quick "thanks," like high-fiving someone as you walk by? Do you forget to praise him at all? Or do you stop to consider all that God has done for you and offer him the praise he deserves?

God gives us too many blessings to count, from providing for our daily needs (food, clothing, and shelter) to offering us eternal salvation through Jesus! Like Mary, are you in awe that the holy, all-powerful God of the universe cares about you? Do you shake your head in wonder that he sent his only Son, Jesus, to die in your place and pay for your sins? Do you marvel at Jesus' resurrection, which proved that God accepted his sacrifice on your behalf?

Don't take God's goodness for granted. Follow Mary's example and praise him! He is worthy of all our worship and thanks.

BATTLE PLAN

Write your own poem or song of praise to God. Include all his blessings that you can remember. If you or someone you know is gifted musically, perhaps you can even put the words to music!

DAY 72

A HERO'S TALE

MESSAGE FROM HEADQUARTERS

There they were, huddled together in a small upper room in Jerusalem. Waiting . . . and praying . . . and praying some more.

It was an exciting time for the small group of believers. Jesus' disciples were there (minus Judas Iscariot, the betrayer), as well as other Christians. So was Mary.

More than 30 years had passed since that glorious night in the Bethlehem manger. Mary had watched her baby boy grow up and lead a remarkable life, filled with powerful preaching and astounding miracles.

> LET ME NOW REMIND YOU, DEAR BROTHERS AND SISTERS, OF THE GOOD NEWS I PREACHED TO YOU BEFORE. YOU WELCOMED IT THEN, AND YOU STILL STAND FIRM IN IT. IT IS THIS GOOD NEWS THAT SAVES YOU IF YOU CONTINUE TO BELIEVE THE MESSAGE I TOLD YOU.
> – 1 CORINTHIANS 15:1-2

Mary hadn't always understood everything about her Son (see Mark 3:20-21). And she must have had a million questions racing through her mind as she stood near the cross during Jesus' crucifixion (see John 19:25).

The next time we read about Mary is in Acts 1. Jesus had gloriously resurrected, appeared to many people, and ascended into heaven. Before he left, Jesus had told his disciples to wait in Jerusalem until God sent the Holy Spirit to them (see Acts 1:4).

Mary joined the disciples in the upper room. Acts 1:14 says, "They all met together and were constantly united in prayer, along with Mary the mother of Jesus, several other women, and the brothers of Jesus."

Mary's presence proved an important fact: she had become a true believer in Christ!

DECODING THE MESSAGE

The Bible doesn't say exactly when, but at some point, Mary went from simply being Jesus' earthly mom to trusting in him for the forgiveness of her sins. That's clear from the faith that led her to the upper room after Jesus' ascension.

True heroes for God must respond in faith to the gospel message (the good news that Jesus died to save us). Mary's life is a great example of that. If anyone could have earned special favor with God, it would've been the mother of Jesus! But Mary, like the rest of us, was still a sinner who needed a Savior.

You've heard the good news about Jesus, too (in this book, for instance). But it's not enough to only hear the message. You have to believe it and accept it. You have to trust in Jesus and give your life to him, just like Mary did.

Will you do it?

BATTLE PLAN

The apostle Paul wanted to make sure the readers of his letter called 1 Corinthians responded to the gospel in faith. Read 1 Corinthians 15:1-8 and pray that God would give you faith in the gospel of Jesus!

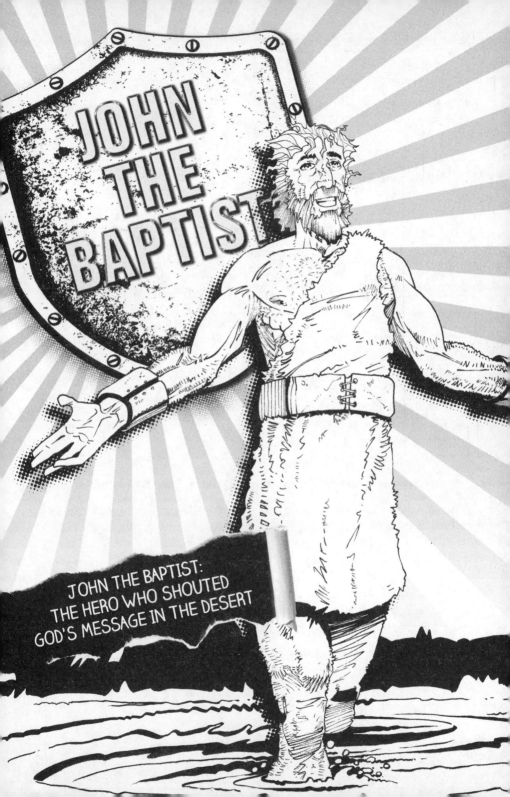

DAY 73

IS WILLING TO SACRIFICE COMFORT TO OBEY GOD.

A HERO'S TALE

Of all the Bible's heroes, John the Baptist might have been the strangest. If John lived in today's world, he probably would've had his own reality TV show.

John could have become a respected Jewish priest like his father, Zechariah. Or he could have earned a comfortable living another way. Instead, John moved away from his loved ones to live in the desert. For clothing, he wore a tunic of "camel hair" tucked into "a leather belt around his waist" (Matthew 3:4). In other words, he wasn't a Gap model.

> **MESSAGE FROM HEADQUARTERS**
>
> OF ALL WHO HAVE EVER LIVED, NONE IS GREATER THAN JOHN THE BAPTIST. YET EVEN THE LEAST PERSON IN THE KINGDOM OF HEAVEN IS GREATER THAN HE IS!
>
> – MATTHEW 11:11

John's diet was weird too. He often ate locusts dipped in honey. Not exactly fine dining.

Then again, John wasn't interested in a life of comfort. His main goal wasn't to take it easy. He was most interested in obeying God.

DECODING THE MESSAGE

We live in a world obsessed with comfort. Many people try to find comfort in money and earthly possessions. Other people seek comfort in relaxation or entertainment. They always seem to be plugged into video games, TV, movies, or music.

There's nothing wrong with enjoying life. But for Christians, life isn't about comfort. It's about glorifying God.

John the Baptist understood this. He realized that it's more important to live a godly life than a comfortable one. So he did hard things for God. He lived in the hot, dusty desert because that's where God sent him to preach the gospel. And he called people to repent of their sins even though it eventually got him killed (see Matthew 14:1-12).

We should be more like John the Baptist. No, that doesn't mean you need to pack your bags for the Sahara or buy the latest camel-hair T-shirt. But you should value obeying God more than treasuring comfort.

BATTLE PLAN

The next time your favorite TV show is on, take that 30 to 60 minutes, instead, to do something kind for someone else. Write an encouraging note to a family member, bake cookies for a friend, or rake someone's leaves. Sacrifice your comfort to show God's love to another.

GOSPEL CONNECTION

No one in history sacrificed comfort more than Jesus Christ. The Son of God left his perfect heavenly home to live a difficult human life in a fallen, sinful world. Jesus didn't even have a regular bed to sleep in (see Matthew 8:20). He gave up heavenly glory to be ridiculed, rejected, and ultimately killed for our sins. All because he loves us!

A TRUE HERO FOR GOD . . . | UNDERSTANDS WHO JESUS REALLY IS.

A HERO'S TALE

John the Baptist—with his camel-hair-and-leather outfits, insect-heavy diet, and bold preaching—was quite a sight to behold. Huge crowds flocked to the Jordan River to hear him speak, be baptized, and gaze in wonder at this powerful, quirky man.

> **MESSAGE FROM HEADQUARTERS**
>
> JOHN SAW JESUS COMING TOWARD HIM AND SAID, "LOOK! THE LAMB OF GOD WHO TAKES AWAY THE SIN OF THE WORLD!"
> – JOHN 1:29

Yes, John was a little unusual, but he wasn't a carnival act. He had a specific purpose, given to him by the Lord. Before John's birth, the angel Gabriel declared that John would "prepare the people for the coming of the Lord" (Luke 1:17). His mission was to reveal God's long-awaited Messiah.

One day as John was baptizing, he looked up and saw Jesus approaching. John's heart raced with excitement. He turned to the crowd, pointed toward Jesus, and shouted, "Look! The Lamb of God who takes away the sin of the world!" (John 1:29). A few minutes later, John told the multitude, "I testify that he is the Chosen One of God" (1:34).

John clearly understood who Jesus was.

DECODING THE MESSAGE

Lots of people today have different ideas about Jesus.

Some people believe Jesus was simply a good teacher or a great prophet, but not divine. Others believe that Jesus was a god, but not equal with God the Father. Still others believe that the life of Jesus (and the Bible in general) is like an Aesop's fable—nothing more than a nice story with good morals. There are also those who don't even believe Jesus existed, and plenty of others don't really care about Jesus one way or the other.

But these opinions of Jesus are all wrong.

We must be very careful to understand who Jesus really is. Nothing is more important in life because it's only by faith in Jesus that we can be made right with God (see John 14:6).

Jesus is the eternal Son of God, fully God and fully man, one with the Father and Holy Spirit, never created and completely sinless. He died as the perfect sacrifice for our sins, resurrected on the third day, and now sits at the Father's right hand in heaven, where one day he will bring all true believers to live with him forever.

But that will happen only for those who, through faith, understand who Jesus really is.

BATTLE PLAN

There's no better way to learn about Jesus than to read the New Testament Gospels—Matthew, Mark, Luke, and John. Each is a factual, God-inspired account of Jesus' earthly life and ministry. Plan to read all four this year. There are 89 chapters in all four Gospels combined. If you read one chapter a day starting with Matthew, you'll be done in less than three months. If you read three chapters a day, you'll finish in less than a month!

A TRUE HERO FOR GOD . . . STANDS UP AGAINST EVIL.

A HERO'S TALE

If he hadn't been a prophet, John the Baptist probably would've made an excellent military general, boxer, or politician. That dude wasn't afraid of anyone.

One day, as he was baptizing people in the Jordan River, John saw the Pharisees and Sadducees approaching. These were the Jewish religious leaders who oversaw the spiritual practices of the people and tried to help them understand the Old Testament law.

MESSAGE FROM HEADQUARTERS

WHO WILL PROTECT ME FROM THE WICKED? WHO WILL STAND UP FOR ME AGAINST EVILDOERS?

– PSALM 94:16

But many of these men were hypocrites, meaning they preached one thing and practiced another. They were arrogant and self-righteous. They were more concerned with following rules than loving God and others. They weren't true followers of God.

These men were also powerful, wealthy, and respected (and sometimes even feared) by the people. To cross them meant big trouble.

That didn't matter to John. When he saw them approaching him one day, he loudly called them a "brood of snakes" and warned them to turn from their hypocrisy and follow God (see Matthew 3:7-12). That took guts!

Later in his ministry, John bravely criticized King Herod, the Roman-appointed ruler of Palestine. Herod was sinfully in love with his brother Philip's wife, Herodias, and had married her after she divorced Philip. John chastised Herod—a godly rebuke that ultimately got him executed.

John had no problem standing up against evil!

DECODING THE MESSAGE

What would you do if you saw a kid calling someone else names or hitting him or her? If you saw another kid lying, cheating, or stealing? If your friend wanted to disobey his parents?

Would you laugh and join in? Ignore the bad behavior? Bad-mouth that person to others? Or would you lovingly try to help him or her do the right thing instead?

Standing up against evil isn't easy. It takes courage and a heart that wants to please God more than man. That's what John the Baptist had. He didn't care what people thought of him. He wanted to obey God above all.

But be careful. Standing up against evil does *not* mean being unkind to others. Just because people sometimes do something wrong, you should never act like you're better than them, speak angrily to them, tattle just to get them in trouble, etc. Even when you disagree with someone who is doing something wrong, you still need to show kindness.

So stand up against evil in a loving way! (But try not to call anyone a brood of snakes.)

BATTLE PLAN

Talk to your parents about what to do when you see someone else doing something wrong. God gave your parents wisdom to help you figure out difficult situations!

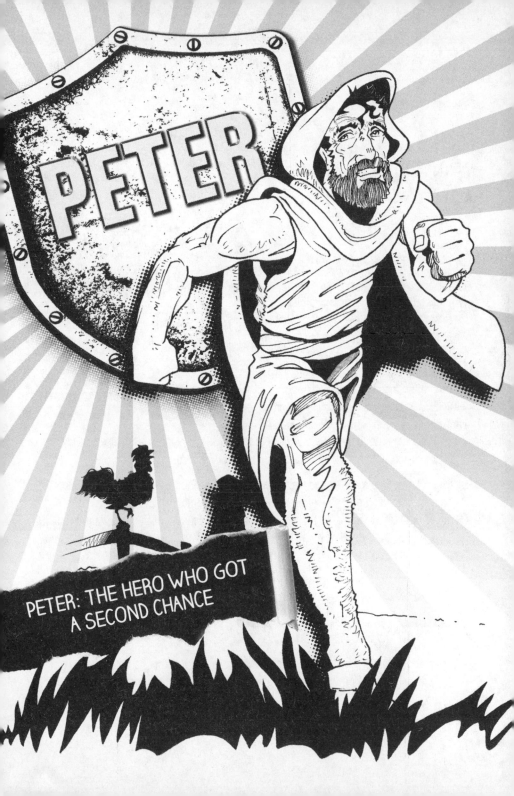

PETER: THE HERO WHO GOT
A SECOND CHANCE

DAY 76

ALWAYS FORGIVES THOSE WHO WRONG HIM.

A HERO'S TALE

Peter desperately wanted to be a hero for God.

When Jesus started his public ministry, traveling throughout Palestine to preach the Good News and perform miracles to prove that he was God's long-awaited Messiah, he chose 12 disciples to accompany him. Among these men, Peter was the natural leader. He was brave, strong willed, and unafraid to speak his mind. If Peter was in your school class, he'd be the kid jumping to answer every question first, whether he was right or wrong.

> **MESSAGE FROM HEADQUARTERS**
>
> MAKE ALLOWANCE FOR EACH OTHER'S FAULTS, AND FORGIVE ANYONE WHO OFFENDS YOU. REMEMBER, THE LORD FORGAVE YOU, SO YOU MUST FORGIVE OTHERS.
> – COLOSSIANS 3:13

One day, Jesus was teaching his disciples about forgiveness. Wanting to look good, Peter asked Jesus, "Lord, how often should I forgive someone who sins against me? Seven times?" (Matthew 18:21). The Jewish religious leaders at the time taught that forgiving someone three times was good enough. So by suggesting seven times, Peter figured he was being superholy.

Jesus' answer must have surprised him: "No, not seven times, but seventy times seven!" (see Matthew 18:22).

DECODING THE MESSAGE

What an interesting answer from Jesus. Does that mean if someone hits you 490 times, you should forgive, but on the 491st time, you can start pounding him? No way!

Jesus picked a really big number like 490 to make this point: you should *always* forgive those who wrong you. It was a lesson the disciples (and we!) needed to hear.

Why should we always forgive? Jesus answered that by telling his disciples a story: there was a man who owed his master a huge sum of money that he could never repay. After the man begged for mercy, the master graciously forgave the entire debt.

But after leaving, the man found one of his fellow servants who owed him a very small amount. Even though the man had just been forgiven a massive debt, he mistreated his fellow servant and threw him in jail. Soon, the master found out and justly punished the unforgiving man (see Matthew 18:23-34).

In Jesus' story, the master represents God, and the two servants represent humans. If we've put our faith in Jesus, God has mercifully forgiven us of a lifetime of sins—an enormous debt that we could never repay. Because we've been forgiven so much, we should always forgive others, too. No matter how (or how many times) anyone wrongs you, it doesn't compare to all your sins against God that he forgives through Jesus.

Peter learned a crucial lesson about forgiveness that day. Hopefully, you did too!

BATTLE PLAN

Read and practice Matthew 18:15. If people sin against you, gently approach them about it and forgive them.

A TRUE HERO FOR GOD . . .   IS GRATEFUL FOR GOD'S PATIENCE.

A HERO'S TALE

MESSAGE FROM HEADQUARTERS

THE LORD IS COMPASSIONATE AND MERCIFUL, SLOW TO GET ANGRY AND FILLED WITH UNFAILING LOVE.

– PSALM 103:8

Peter was overwhelmed with remorse. Tears streamed down his cheeks. Scared, confused, and grief stricken, he fled from the courtyard of the high priest.

He had just denied his Lord three times.

As one of the disciples, Peter had spent the previous three years with Jesus. He had listened to Jesus' teachings, seen dozens of amazing miracles, and put his faith in Jesus as God's Savior.

Then came that fateful night when Jesus was arrested in the garden of Gethsemane. To save his own skin, Peter deserted Jesus with the rest of the disciples, then claimed three times that he didn't know Jesus. It was a huge failure on Peter's part.

But this was only one of many sinful blunders by Peter. He often misunderstood Jesus' teachings and spoke or acted without thinking. Once, he scolded Jesus (see Matthew 16:21-23), and in Gethsemane, he even tried to kill a man (see John 18:10). Peter was a big mess.

Yet Jesus still loved him. After Jesus' resurrection, he forgave and restored Peter despite his denials (see John 21). Peter eventually became one of the key leaders of the early church and a powerful witness for Jesus. He even wrote 1 and 2 Peter, two great books of the Bible.

Peter is a great example of God's patience toward us!

DECODING THE MESSAGE

It's easy to pick on Peter since the Bible mentions so many of his mistakes. But honestly, we're all more like Peter than we probably care to admit.

Have you ever lied, stolen, cheated, pouted, complained, shown impatience, disobeyed your parents, been selfish with your toys, yelled at someone, hit a sibling or friend, or called someone a name? Of course you have. We all have. Peter was a big sinner, and so are you.

But here's the good news: God is patient with you, just like he was with Peter! God is not a three-strikes-and-you're-out type of God. He lovingly offers us many chances to repent and follow him.

Peter knew this better than anyone. In his second letter, he wrote that God "is being patient. . . . He does not want anyone to be destroyed" (2 Peter 3:9).

Let's make something clear, though: God's patience is not a free pass to do whatever we want. Christians have a responsibility to obey God and imitate Jesus. But it *does* mean that God is a loving, patient God. He's not going to zap you because you mess up. He's going to lovingly speak to your heart and lead you toward godliness, if you're willing.

Praise God for his patience!

BATTLE PLAN

Read all of Psalm 103. Then thank God for his patience toward you.

DAY 78

A HERO'S TALE

You know the stories of Spider-Man and the Incredible Hulk, right? They were both ordinary men who accidently transformed into powerful superheroes.

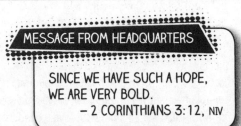

MESSAGE FROM HEADQUARTERS

SINCE WE HAVE SUCH A HOPE, WE ARE VERY BOLD.
— 2 CORINTHIANS 3:12, NIV

The hero story of the apostle Peter is a bit different. Yes, Peter radically changed into a hero, too, but unlike those Marvel Comics characters, he was a real person and his transformation was no accident. (And if you want to get nitpicky about it, Peter didn't spin webs or turn green, either.)

In the Gospel of Matthew, the last specific reference to Peter is his three denials of Jesus. It was the worst failure of Peter's life. He certainly didn't seem prepared to do great things for God.

But in Acts 2, less than two months later, we see a completely different Peter. Restored by Jesus and filled with the Holy Spirit, Peter preached a powerful gospel message to a huge crowd in Jerusalem on the Day of Pentecost. As a result, about 3,000 people put their faith in Christ! Later, when the Jewish religious leaders commanded him to stop speaking about Jesus, Peter courageously refused, choosing to obey God instead. He then "preached the word of God with boldness" elsewhere (Acts 4:31).

By God's power, Peter radically changed from a frightened denier into a bold preacher!

DECODING THE MESSAGE

Boldness is a funny thing. Some people have it naturally. Most people don't. Which kind of person are you?

Either way, the Bible calls all Christians to boldly share their faith. The book of Acts alone mentions boldness at least eight times when it talks about the apostles sharing their faith with others. In Matthew 5:13-16, Jesus refers to his followers as "the light of the world" and "a city on a hilltop." In other words, we are to shine brightly and boldly around unbelievers as a witness that Jesus loves them.

Then of course, there's the famous great commission in Matthew 28:19-20, where Jesus tells us, "Go and make disciples of all the nations, baptizing them in the name of the Father and the Son and the Holy Spirit. Teach these new disciples to obey all the commands I have given you."

The message is clear: God wants us to boldly share our faith with others. Do you lack boldness? That's okay! It's not always easy for us to do this. Ask God for strength, and he will give you heavenly power. He did it for Peter, and he'll do it for you!

BATTLE PLAN

Do you know someone who isn't a Christian? Pray to God for boldness, then speak to that person about Jesus.

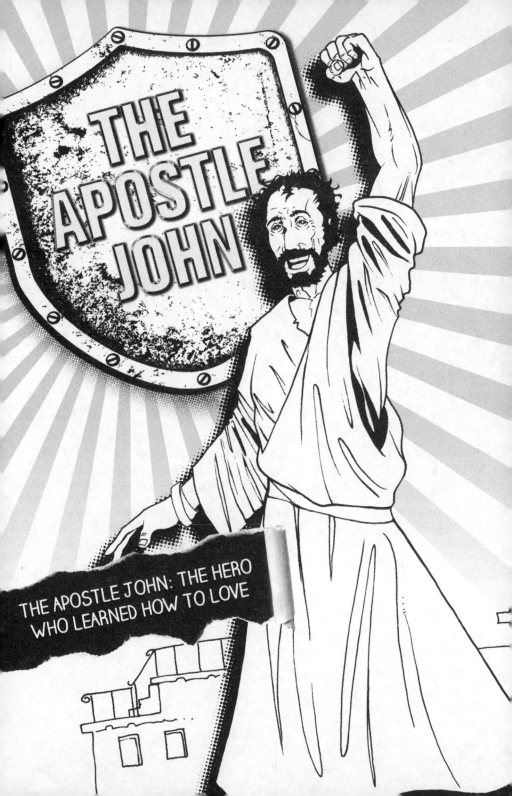

A TRUE HERO FOR GOD . . . ║ DOES NOT JUDGE OTHERS.

A HERO'S TALE

Like Peter and Andrew, John and James were fishermen brothers who became disciples of Jesus. Early on, Jesus gave John and James the nickname "Sons of Thunder" (Mark 3:17). It was likely a reference to their strong personalities and hot tempers.

> **MESSAGE FROM HEADQUARTERS**
>
> DO NOT JUDGE OTHERS, AND YOU WILL NOT BE JUDGED.
> — MATTHEW 7:1

We see these traits of John and James in Luke 9:51-56. As Jesus and the disciples were heading toward Jerusalem, they stopped briefly in a Samaritan village. The Samaritans were a partly Jewish ethnic group that regular Jews hated.

The Samaritan townspeople rudely rejected Jesus and his disciples. That didn't sit well with the Sons of Thunder. So they asked Jesus, "Lord, should we call down fire from heaven to burn them up?" (Wow, don't get on John's and James's bad side!)

The thought hadn't even crossed Jesus' mind. He "turned and rebuked" John and James. The Sons of Thunder learned an important lesson that day.

DECODING THE MESSAGE

John and James had sinfully judged the Samaritans. They forgot what Jesus had taught them earlier in the Sermon on the Mount: "Do not judge others, and you will not be judged. For you will be treated as you treat others. The standard you use in judging is the standard by which you will be judged" (Matthew 7:1-2).

To judge others means to pronounce them guilty of something before God. But none of us has the right to do that. We are all sinners. It's not our place to proudly look down on someone else's faults, because we've got plenty of our own. That's why, in Matthew 7:3, Jesus said, "Why worry about a speck in your friend's eye when you have a log in your own?"

Are you allowed to graciously help someone overcome a sin or bad habit? Of course! But don't view yourself as better than the other person when doing it.

John learned his lesson. Years later, he became one of the great leaders of the early church. He also wrote the Gospel of John and three Epistles (or letters to churches)—1, 2, and 3 John. In fact, 1 John is all about loving God and others. And true love doesn't judge people.

Clearly, John had learned not to judge others with a sinful heart.

BATTLE PLAN

Read any (or all!) of the following passages on judging others: Matthew 7:1-5; Luke 6:37-42; Romans 2:1-16; Romans 14:10-13; and James 4:11-12.

GOSPEL CONNECTION

The Bible says God, the Righteous Judge, will judge everyone when they die. (He can do this because he is holy.) But we can avoid the punishment our sins deserve through repentance and faith in Jesus. God's Son died and rose again to save us from God's just judgment!

DAY 80

HAS FAITH IN THE SAVING POWER OF JESUS' RESURRECTION.

A HERO'S TALE

Usain Bolt can fly.

At the 2008 and 2012 Olympics, the Jamaican superstar proved he was the fastest man on the planet, winning gold medals in the 100 and 200 meters and the 4x100-meter relay in world-record times.

Good thing Bolt didn't live in first-century Palestine, though. He might have lost a footrace to the apostle John, at least on that miraculous Sunday after Jesus died.

MESSAGE FROM HEADQUARTERS

IF YOU OPENLY DECLARE THAT JESUS IS LORD AND BELIEVE IN YOUR HEART THAT GOD RAISED HIM FROM THE DEAD, YOU WILL BE SAVED.
– ROMANS 10:9

That morning, Mary Magdalene and a few other women went to the tomb where their Lord's body had been placed. But when they arrived, they found the stone at the entrance rolled away and the tomb empty. Mary hurried back to tell Peter and John. Alarmed and confused, the two disciples sprinted to the tomb, but John arrived before Peter. You've never seen a man in a tunic and sandals run so fast. Watch out, Usain.

Peter entered the tomb first and saw nothing, except the burial cloths that had been wrapped around Jesus. "Then," John 20:8 says, "the disciple who had reached the tomb first [John] also went in, and he saw and believed."

Later that evening, Jesus appeared in person to the disciples. He had truly risen from the dead! Over the next 40 days, John and the disciples saw Jesus many other times before he ascended into heaven.

John had seen and believed. Many years later, he wrote about Jesus' life, death, and resurrection in his Gospel "so that you may continue to believe that Jesus is the

Messiah, the Son of God, and that by believing in him you will have life by the power of his name" (John 20:31).

DECODING THE MESSAGE

Jesus was a real, historical person who lived in Palestine in the early part of the first century AD. Many people—even non-Christian religious scholars—admit that. But simply believing Jesus existed isn't good enough.

The Bible says we must put our faith in the saving power of Jesus' resurrection. As the apostle Paul said in Philippians 3:10, "I want to know Christ and experience the mighty power that raised him from the dead."

Why is this so important? Because Jesus' resurrection proved that

- he truly was the Son of God;
- he defeated sin and death forever; and
- God accepted his sacrifice on our behalf.

You can't truly be a Christian—a follower of Christ—without believing these truths.

John was an eyewitness of Jesus' life, death, and resurrection. He wrote his Gospel so you would believe.

Do you?

BATTLE PLAN

Celebrating Jesus' resurrection isn't just for Easter. Read one (or all) of the Gospel accounts of Jesus' resurrection and praise him for rising to life again!

DAY 81

UNDERSTANDS YOU CAN'T LOVE GOD AND HATE OTHERS.

A HERO'S TALE

When you watch a superhero movie, what do you want to see? Action? Yes. Fights? Yes. Explosions? Yes. How about awesome gadgets, shocking stunts, and amazing special effects? Yes, yes, and yes!

What about love?

Ewwww, gross! No way!

> **MESSAGE FROM HEADQUARTERS**
>
> DEAR FRIENDS, LET US CONTINUE TO LOVE ONE ANOTHER, FOR LOVE COMES FROM GOD.
>
> – 1 JOHN 4:7

C'mon, who wants to see kissing in a superhero movie, right? And for that matter, who ever heard of a movie where the superhero and supervillain love each other and never fight? Talk about boring!

But before you get too disgusted, consider this: the apostle John, a great hero of the Bible, talked about love all the time. No, not the romantic, smoochy stuff. John talked about God's love toward us and the love we are to show others. In fact, you could say 1 John is a love letter. You can't read more than a few sentences in the book without seeing the word *love*.

You see, true heroes for God understand you can't love God and hate others.

DECODING THE MESSAGE

Be honest: there's someone in your life who really irritates you, isn't there? Perhaps it's a sibling or that annoying kid in school or a neighborhood bully.

It's tough to be around difficult people. Maybe you just plain hate them. After all, it's okay to hate if someone deserves it, right?

Wrong.

The Bible teaches us to be kind to others (see Matthew 7:12; Ephesians 4:32; and Philippians 2:3-4, among other verses). But the Bible goes further than that. It says that you can't hate someone else *and* love God. It's just not possible.

Listen to the straightforward words of 1 John 4:20-21: "Whoever claims to love God yet hates a brother or sister is a liar. For whoever does not love their brother and sister, whom they have seen, cannot love God, whom they have not seen. And he has given us this command: Anyone who loves God must also love their brother and sister" (NIV).

As we learned in the first devotional on the apostle John, he was once filled with hate and anger (see Luke 9:51-55). But by watching Jesus, he learned how to love.

God's Word makes it clear: loving God and hating others don't mix. That's because loving God means being like him and obeying his commands. God is love, not hate, and he commands *us* to love others too. It's that simple.

So feel free to turn off that lovey-dovey superhero movie. But don't turn off your love for others.

BATTLE PLAN

Do you feel hatred toward some people? Ask for God's forgiveness, ask for theirs, and make an effort to do something kind to them.

GOSPEL CONNECTION

Aren't you glad that God shows us love instead of hate? His greatest expression of love for us was through his Son, Jesus. Romans 5:8 says, "God showed his great love for us by sending Christ to die for us while we were still sinners." If that's not true love, nothing is!

PAUL: THE HERO WHO WENT FROM SUPERVILLAIN TO SUPERMISSIONARY

A TRUE HERO FOR GOD . . .

REJOICES THAT GOD CAN SAVE THE WORST OF SINNERS.

A HERO'S TALE

An evil smile spread across Saul's face.

He watched as large rocks—thrown by a hateful, angry mob—flew through the air and slammed into Stephen's body. Stephen, a godly leader in the early church, was being stoned to death for his faith. And Saul, a young Pharisee, couldn't have been happier. As Stephen's life ended, Saul nodded in sinister approval. (See Acts 6:8–8:1 for the full story.)

Inspired by Stephen's death, wicked Saul made it his life mission to destroy Christianity, a new faith in the first century AD (originally called "the Way") comprised of people who believed Jesus was God's Savior. Like a hungry wolf hunting his prey, he traveled far and wide, searching for followers of Jesus to imprison.

But God had other plans for Saul.

One day, as Saul was traveling toward the city of Damascus to persecute the local believers, the risen Jesus suddenly appeared to Saul, knocking him down and blinding him with brilliant glory. That moment changed Saul forever.

MESSAGE FROM HEADQUARTERS

HERE IS A TRUSTWORTHY SAYING THAT DESERVES FULL ACCEPTANCE: CHRIST JESUS CAME INTO THE WORLD TO SAVE SINNERS – OF WHOM I AM THE WORST. BUT FOR THAT VERY REASON I WAS SHOWN MERCY SO THAT IN ME, THE WORST OF SINNERS, CHRIST JESUS MIGHT DISPLAY HIS IMMENSE PATIENCE AS AN EXAMPLE FOR THOSE WHO WOULD BELIEVE IN HIM AND RECEIVE ETERNAL LIFE.
– 1 TIMOTHY 1:15-16, NIV

Saul (who changed his name to Paul) went from a devoted Jesus hater to a devoted Jesus follower. He dedicated his life to spreading the gospel worldwide, taking at least three missionary trips and writing 13 New Testament books.

By God's power, Paul was a completely new man!

DECODING THE MESSAGE

Think about your life. How many times have you sinned? If you're honest, it's too many to count.

Now think about the worst things you've done: Lying? Cheating? Stealing? Hitting? Screaming in anger? Even worse? It's probably a pretty terrible list.

But before you get discouraged, remember Paul. He once *hated* Jesus (because if you hate Jesus' disciples, you hate Jesus, too). Yet God saved Paul and radically transformed his life.

Now look at today's verse. Later in life, Paul admitted that he was the "worst of sinners." But God was greater than Paul's sins. He can radically transform even the worst of us.

He can do that for you, too. It doesn't matter who you are or how bad a sinner you think you are. God loves you, and he wants to save you and use you for his glory. Trust in the risen Jesus, like Paul did, and let God start changing you, too!

BATTLE PLAN

To learn more about Paul's remarkable conversion, read Acts 9:1-31 and Galatians 1:11-24.

DAY 83

REMAINS COMMITTED TO GOD HIS WHOLE LIFE.

A HERO'S TALE

Let's talk about the Biebs.

Ever since his YouTube videos were discovered in 2008, Justin Bieber has been one of pop music's hottest stars. Young boys want to be like him. Young girls squeal when they see him. His legions of devoted followers call themselves "Beliebers."

> **MESSAGE FROM HEADQUARTERS**
>
> I HAVE FOUGHT THE GOOD FIGHT, I HAVE FINISHED THE RACE, AND I HAVE REMAINED FAITHFUL.
> – 2 TIMOTHY 4:7

But one day, belieb—uh, believe—it or not, Biebermania will be a distant memory. That's the way these things go. Before Bieber, boy bands *NSYNC, Backstreet Boys, and the Jonas Brothers were wildly popular. But you probably don't remember them.

In the '80s, it was New Kids on the Block, New Edition, and Menudo. In the '70s, it was The Jackson 5. In the '60s, it was The Beatles and The Monkees.

You get the point. Fads are fun and exciting, but they don't last.

Throughout his long ministry as a missionary, preacher, and church builder, the apostle Paul warned people not to treat Christianity like a short-lived spiritual fad. He often compared life to a long race. In 1 Corinthians 9:24, he said, "Don't you realize that in a race everyone runs, but only one person gets the prize? So run to win!"

DECODING THE MESSAGE

Christianity is not like a hot new music album that you eventually get tired of and delete from your MP3 player. It's not just a quick prayer you pray. No, following Jesus is a lifelong commitment. True heroes for God remain committed to him their whole lives.

During his life, Paul saw many people who claimed to be Christians fall away (see 2 Timothy 4:10). But Paul never stopped living for Jesus. This requires perseverance, faithfulness, and much prayer.

You are just starting your journey of faith. You'll encounter many problems in life. At times, you might want to abandon your faith. But stay strong. God is faithful. He will never stop loving you, so don't ever stop following him.

Remember, too, that you can't be a true hero for God on your own. You need God's help. So read his Word daily. Pray to him continually. Surround yourself with other believers who love God too.

By the end of his life, Paul said, "I have fought the good fight, I have finished the race, and I have remained faithful" (2 Timothy 4:7). Will you be able to say the same thing?

BATTLE PLAN

Start a spiritual journal. Write down what you're learning about following Jesus, how you're doing, and spiritual questions you have. It's a great way to track your commitment to God over time.

A TRUE HERO FOR GOD . . .

PERSEVERES THROUGH TRIALS IN FAITH.

A HERO'S TALE

The apostle Paul had a difficult life. We're talking advanced-placement-chemistry difficult. His life included so many trials, you'd need a calculator to count them all.

In 2 Corinthians 11, Paul lists some of the troubles he faced as a follower of Jesus:

- multiple imprisonments
- whipped 39 times on five separate occasions
- beaten with rods three times
- shipwrecked three times, including 24 hours of floating in the open sea
- many days without food or water

> ### MESSAGE FROM HEADQUARTERS
>
> GOD BLESSES THOSE WHO PATIENTLY ENDURE TESTING AND TEMPTATION. AFTERWARD THEY WILL RECEIVE THE CROWN OF LIFE THAT GOD HAS PROMISED TO THOSE WHO LOVE HIM.
> – JAMES 1:12

Later in his letter to the Corinthians, Paul also says God gave him a mysterious "thorn in my flesh . . . to torment me" (2 Corinthians 12:7). When Paul pleaded for God to remove it, God simply answered, "My grace is all you need. My power works best in weakness" (12:9).

DECODING THE MESSAGE

This life is full of trouble. No doubt about that.

God never promised his children a trouble-free life. In fact, it's quite the opposite. In John 16:33, Jesus promised his disciples, "Here on earth you will have many trials and sorrows."

Sometimes, our troubles are our own fault (a lie you've told that makes matters worse). Other times, it's someone else's fault (a neighborhood bully) or simply life in a fallen, imperfect world (getting sick). And sometimes God allows us to go through trouble without explanation (the death of a loved one).

Whatever the trials are, the key is to persevere through them with faith in God. To "persevere" means to persist, or continue, despite difficulty or discouragement.

Paul knew that the secret to persevering through trials was trusting in the Lord. God is bigger than any problem, and he loves you. He won't let the trial last forever. But he does want your trust.

God's words to Paul are true for you, too: "My grace is all you need. My power works best in weakness." Trials are meant to reveal our weakness and God's strength and to build our faith in him.

BATTLE PLAN

Are you going through a rough time? Read James 1:2-4 and 1 Peter 1:6-7. Then put your faith into action by writing a thank-you note to God for the trial you're facing and what he is teaching you.

GOSPEL CONNECTION

Did you know that even Jesus had to persevere through trials? His human life was full of hardships (see Isaiah 53; Matthew 8:20), and before his crucifixion, he even had to pray to God the Father for strength in the garden of Gethsemane (see Luke 22:39-46). But he endured all difficulties perfectly and won salvation for us through his victorious death and resurrection!

DAY 85

BELIEVES JESUS CAME TO EARTH AS FULLY GOD AND FULLY MAN.

A HERO'S TALE

Have you read The Chronicles of Narnia? Author C. S. Lewis's beloved book series tells the story of a magical, make-believe world called Narnia, ruled by the great lion Aslan, where a family of British children encounter many exciting adventures.

Narnia is filled with mythological beings that are half human, half animal—like fauns, centaurs, and Minotaurs. It's fun to read about these creatures, and it's even cooler to see them come to life in the movies!

MESSAGE FROM HEADQUARTERS

LOOK! THE VIRGIN WILL CONCEIVE A CHILD! SHE WILL GIVE BIRTH TO A SON, AND THEY WILL CALL HIM IMMANUEL, WHICH MEANS "GOD IS WITH US."
– MATTHEW 1:23

Did you know the Bible also tells the story of a person who is more than human? His identity might surprise you.

His name is Jesus.

DECODING THE MESSAGE

Jesus' life didn't begin in the Bethlehem manger. In fact, Jesus had no beginning at all. Jesus is God, and he has always existed with God the Father and God the Spirit, the other two parts of the Holy Trinity, according to John 1:1-2. As the Son of God, Jesus lived in heaven before human life, or time itself, began.

Jesus' birth on earth was a wonderful miracle. Bible scholars refer to Jesus' human birth as "the Incarnation."

This marvelous mystery is captured in the name "Immanuel," one of the titles given to Jesus in Isaiah 7:14 and Matthew 1:23. *Immanuel* means "God is with us." In other words, God the Son came to earth as a man to live among us.

But unlike Narnia's mythological creatures, Jesus didn't come to earth as half man and half something else. He came as *fully* God and *fully* man.

This amazing truth can be hard to understand. But it's so important to believe. As the God-man, Jesus experienced everything we do as humans (joy, sadness, laughter, disappointment, pain, etc.) but remained perfectly sinless. Jesus lived a real human life, and he did it with complete holiness. That's why he, and no one else, could die for our sins on the cross. Incredible!

The story of a little baby born 2,000 years ago in a Bethlehem manger is much more than a nice Christmas tale to read in front of the fireplace. The Incarnation was the greatest miracle in history and an amazing hero story! It's the story of God becoming man, all because he loves you.

BATTLE PLAN

To better understand the Incarnation and Jesus' eternal nature, perform a brief exercise: read John 1:1-3; Colossians 1:16-17; Hebrews 1:1-2; and Revelation 22:13. These passages all show that Jesus has always existed. Bethlehem was not the start of his life, only the beginning of his humanity. Now, go back and read Genesis 1—the Bible's opening account of God creating the universe—but do it remembering that Jesus was right there with the Father, active in all creation. Amazing!

A TRUE HERO FOR GOD . . . | BELIEVES JESUS SAVES US FROM SIN AND DEATH.

A HERO'S TALE

Mariano Rivera sure knows how to save.

The longtime New York Yankees closer ended his career in 2013 as Major League Baseball's all-time saves leader with 652. A "save" in baseball is awarded to the last pitcher on the winning team who enters a game and holds a lead of three runs or less.

Rivera, a 12-time All-Star and a 5-time World Series winner, has dominated the ninth inning like no other pitcher in history. Without question, he is the greatest closer ever.

> **MESSAGE FROM HEADQUARTERS**
>
> THIS IS HOW GOD LOVED THE WORLD: HE GAVE HIS ONE AND ONLY SON, SO THAT EVERYONE WHO BELIEVES IN HIM WILL NOT PERISH BUT HAVE ETERNAL LIFE. GOD SENT HIS SON INTO THE WORLD NOT TO JUDGE THE WORLD, BUT TO SAVE THE WORLD THROUGH HIM.
> – JOHN 3:16-17

Still, when it comes to the most important version of saving, no one compares with Jesus Christ!

The Bible often refers to Jesus as the Savior. John 4:42 calls Jesus "the Savior of the world." Acts 5:31 says he is "Prince and Savior," while Acts 13:23 refers to him as "the Savior Jesus" (NIV). Don't forget Titus 2:13, which mentions "our great God and Savior, Jesus Christ."

Scripture makes it very clear: Jesus came to earth to save us.

DECODING THE MESSAGE

Yes, Jesus is the Savior. But what, exactly, does he save us from? Space aliens? Man-eating sharks? Eating cauliflower for dinner every night?

No, Jesus came to save us from sin and death!

Lots of people don't realize they need to be saved from anything. But the Bible says that every human is a sinner (see Romans 3:23), meaning everyone breaks God's laws. Left to ourselves, we would all be doomed to hell because sin separates us from God (see Romans 6:23). We need a Savior, someone to take away our sins forever.

That person is Jesus.

As the sinless Son of God, he was uniquely qualified to pay the penalty that we deserve (see Hebrews 9:11-14). But he didn't just die for us—he came back to life! And by doing so, he conquered sin and death once for all (see 1 Corinthians 15). Sin and death have no power over him, and through faith in Jesus, we can defeat them too!

We will still die a physical death, yes, but if you trust in Jesus as your Savior, you will avoid what the Bible calls the "second death" (hell) and live forever with Jesus in heaven.

Jesus is a mighty Savior!

BATTLE PLAN

Since we're talking about "saving" today, here's a helpful tip: Are you saving money to buy something special? Every time you drop a coin in your piggy bank, thank Jesus for dying to save you!

DAY 87

EXCITEDLY LOOKS FORWARD TO JESUS' RETURN.

A HERO'S TALE

Think about your favorite day of the year. Is it your birthday? Christmas? The last day of school? Groundhog Day? (Ha, ha.)

Whatever it is, it's a wonderful day that you look forward to all year. You've probably got goose bumps now just thinking about it.

Guess what? A day is coming that is infinitely greater than your favorite day: the return of Jesus!

MESSAGE FROM HEADQUARTERS

HE WHO IS THE FAITHFUL WITNESS TO ALL THESE THINGS SAYS, "YES, I AM COMING SOON!" AMEN! COME, LORD JESUS!
— REVELATION 22:20

Read how 1 Thessalonians 4:16-17 describes it: "The Lord himself will come down from heaven with a commanding shout, with the voice of the archangel, and with the trumpet call of God. First, the believers who have died will rise from their graves. Then, together with them, we who are still alive and remain on the earth will be caught up in the clouds to meet the Lord in the air. Then we will be with the Lord forever."

Wow!

DECODING THE MESSAGE

There's no future event that should excite us more than the return of Jesus. It will be a day like none other, with more cosmic fireworks than the biggest Fourth of July celebration you can imagine (see Matthew 24:27-31).

The Bible doesn't provide every detail about Jesus' return. But we do know this much: currently, Jesus is in heaven with God the Father, preparing an eternal home for all believers (see John 14:2-3). One day—and no one knows when (see Mark 13:32)— Jesus will return to earth for the final time. His mission will be

- to destroy Satan and all evil (see Revelation 20:1-10);
- to punish the wicked and reward the righteous (see Matthew 25:31-46); and
- to bring an end to this world (see 2 Peter 3:10) and begin his eternal Kingdom (see Revelation 21).

Jesus' return will mark the beginning of eternity. Those who have trusted in Jesus will have the inexpressible joy of spending forever with God the Father and the risen Lord Jesus in heaven.

As the apostle John wrote in today's verse, "Come, Lord Jesus!"

BATTLE PLAN

To learn more about Jesus' second coming, check out the following passages:

- Matthew 24:23-51
- 1 Corinthians 15:50-57
- Philippians 3:20-21
- 1 Thessalonians 4:13–5:3
- 2 Thessalonians 1:5–2:12
- 2 Peter 3:1-13
- Revelation 19:11-21

GOSPEL CONNECTION

While Jesus' return should excite his followers, it should greatly trouble those who don't know him. His first coming was for salvation (dying for our sins). His second coming is for judgment (bringing the righteous to heaven and sending unbelievers to hell). When Jesus returns, it will be too late for unbelievers. Have you put your faith in Jesus? If not, don't wait another day! Confess your sins, trust in Jesus, and receive God's forgiveness.

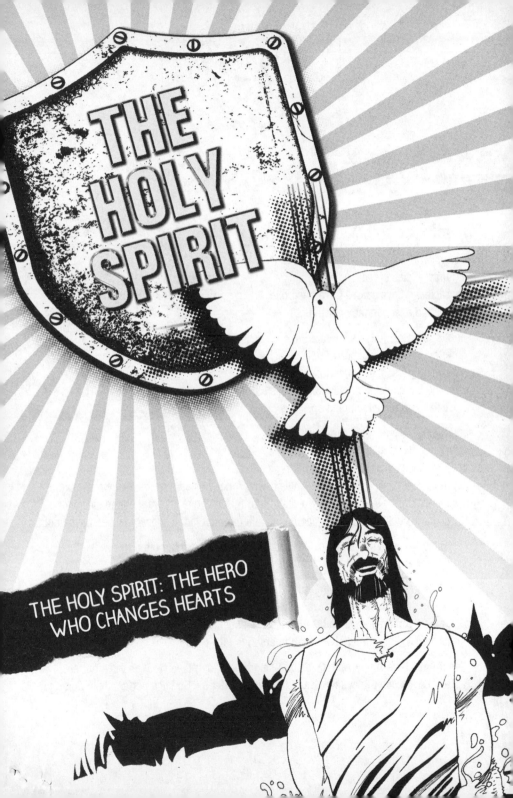

DAY 88

BELIEVES IN THE SAVING WORK OF THE HOLY SPIRIT.

A HERO'S TALE

American history is filled with folklore— legendary tales of real and fictional characters whose stories have been told, retold, and exaggerated over time.

One of the most famous characters in American folklore is Johnny Appleseed. He was a real person, but quite misunderstood. Over the centuries, fact and fiction in his life story have gotten all jumbled up.

Johnny Appleseed's real name was John Chapman. He was born in Massachusetts in 1774, and yes, he did plant apple trees in Pennsylvania, Ohio, Indiana, and Illinois during America's early years. Was he an animal lover? Yes. Did he sleep next to wolves? Doubtful. Did he really wear coffee sacks for shirts and a cooking pot on his head and walk barefoot in the snow? Maybe, maybe not.

The Bible tells of a person who, like John Chapman, is real but often misunderstood too. It's the Holy Spirit.

The Bible has plenty to say about the Holy Spirit. He can't be seen, but he is not a ghost or some sort of make-believe creature. He is the eternal third person of the triune God, along with God the Father and God the Son (Jesus). God is one being, but three distinct persons with different functions. Each person is fully God.

This is called the Trinity. And if it's confusing to you, don't worry. Even the smartest Bible scholars don't fully understand the Trinity. After all, God is a perfect, holy God and

> **MESSAGE FROM HEADQUARTERS**
>
> [GOD] SAVED US, NOT BECAUSE OF THE RIGHTEOUS THINGS WE HAD DONE, BUT BECAUSE OF HIS MERCY. HE WASHED AWAY OUR SINS, GIVING US A NEW BIRTH AND NEW LIFE THROUGH THE HOLY SPIRIT.
>
> – TITUS 3:5

we are imperfect humans with limited knowledge. But if the Bible says it, we must believe it's true.

DECODING THE MESSAGE

Why is it so important for us to understand the Holy Spirit? Because we can't be saved from our sins without him.

In John 3, Jesus told Nicodemus, a confused Jewish teacher, that no one can be saved without being "born again" (John 3:3) and "born of the Spirit" (3:8). In other words, becoming a Christian is more than just praying a prayer or "asking Jesus into your heart." It's about God's Spirit changing us from the inside out. He does that by regenerating (or renewing) our sinful hearts and bringing us to the point where we repent (turn) from our sins and put our faith in Jesus.

No one else can accomplish these amazing transformations inside of us—only the Holy Spirit. Without the Spirit pulling us toward Jesus, we wouldn't even know we needed to be saved!

Praise God for the work of his saving Spirit!

BATTLE PLAN

Read the story of Jesus teaching Nicodemus about salvation and God's Spirit in John 3:1-21. If you don't understand all of it, that's okay! Ask your parents to explain it to you.

A TRUE HERO FOR GOD . . .   OBEYS THE HOLY SPIRIT'S LEADING.

A HERO'S TALE

You've seen the Walt Disney movie *Pinocchio*, right?

It's the story of a wooden puppet who comes to life, thanks to a magical Blue Fairy, and goes on a quest to become a real boy, just like his creator, Geppetto the wood-carver, has wished. The Blue Fairy assigns Jiminy Cricket as Pinocchio's conscience to help the puppet learn right from wrong as he experiences the big, scary world outside his doors. Before leaving, the Blue Fairy says, "Now remember, Pinocchio, be a good boy, and always let your conscience be your guide."

> **MESSAGE FROM HEADQUARTERS**
>
> [JESUS SAID,] "I WILL ASK THE FATHER, AND HE WILL GIVE YOU ANOTHER HELPER, TO BE WITH YOU FOREVER, EVEN THE SPIRIT OF TRUTH, WHOM THE WORLD CANNOT RECEIVE, BECAUSE IT NEITHER SEES HIM NOR KNOWS HIM. YOU KNOW HIM, FOR HE DWELLS WITH YOU AND WILL BE IN YOU."
> – JOHN 14:16-17, ESV

If you're a Christian, you have someone to guide your life, too. But fortunately, it's someone far better than a chirping insect. You have God's own Spirit!

As we learned in yesterday's devotion, the Holy Spirit's work is essential in our salvation. But the Spirit doesn't leave us after that. He lives inside us!

DECODING THE MESSAGE

Read that again: God's Spirit actually lives inside all followers of Jesus. What an amazing truth!

Before Jesus ascended back to heaven, he promised his disciples (and all other Christians afterward) that he would send the "Helper," or the Holy Spirit, to be with them forever (see today's verse). It's one of the greatest blessings of following Jesus.

God isn't a faraway God. He's not a God who sits way off in heaven and doesn't care about his children. No! He loves us so much that when we trust in his Son, he actually sends his own Spirit to live in us.

Jesus called the Holy Spirit the "Helper" because that's just what he does. The Spirit helps us by

- showing us our need for a Savior;
- telling us what's right and wrong;
- making us more like Jesus;
- giving us different abilities to serve God;
- praying on our behalf; and
- much more.

If that's not a Helper, what is?

So forget tiny cartoon crickets! That's just Disney make-believe. When you feel that tugging in your heart to do what's right, that's the Holy Spirit talking to you. Let *him* be your guide!

BATTLE PLAN

Look up "Holy Spirit" in a study Bible concordance to learn more about the incredible third person of the Trinity. Ask your parents for help, if needed.

DAY 90

BELIEVES THE HOLY SPIRIT INSPIRED ALL SCRIPTURE.

A HERO'S TALE

What's your favorite book of all time?

Maybe something from the Harry Potter or Chronicles of Narnia series? How about The Hunger Games or Diary of a Wimpy Kid? Or maybe it's one of the classics from your youth, such as *Curious George, The Cat in the Hat,* or *The Little Engine That Could*? Don't be afraid to admit it. Your secret is safe.

Adult critics have debated the world's greatest book for centuries. In 2007, J. Peder Zane, a writer and editor in North Carolina, asked 125 of the world's top living authors what the 10 greatest books of all time were and published his own book about it.

> **MESSAGE FROM HEADQUARTERS**
>
> NO PROPHECY IN SCRIPTURE EVER CAME FROM THE PROPHET'S OWN UNDERSTANDING, OR FROM HUMAN INITIATIVE. NO, THOSE PROPHETS WERE MOVED BY THE HOLY SPIRIT, AND THEY SPOKE FROM GOD.
> – 2 PETER 1:20-21

Number one on the list was *Anna Karenina* by 19th-century Russian author Leo Tolstoy. You probably haven't read that yet. It's loooooong.

Zane's list was interesting, but the top choice was way off. History's greatest book didn't come from a human author. The Holy Spirit wrote it.

It's the Bible.

DECODING THE MESSAGE

The Bible wins because it's God's perfect master-piece. From Genesis to Revelation, the Bible is a fascinating (and completely true) love story of how a holy God mercifully sacrificed his own Son to save sinners like us.

Human men wrote the Bible's words, but God's Spirit directed every single pen stroke. As today's verse from 2 Peter says, the Bible's human authors all "were moved by the Holy Spirit" as they wrote.

It's fitting that this is the last devotion in this book. After all, there's nothing better you can do in life than to believe the Bible's Spirit-inspired words.

So as you put down this devotion, pick up God's Word once again. Read it. Memorize it. Like a dry sponge soaks up water, let its eternal truths fill your soul. No other book offers the life-changing words of God's salvation.

The apostle Peter so wonderfully put it while speaking to Jesus in John 6:68-69: "Lord, to whom would we go? You have the words that give eternal life. We believe, and we know you are the Holy One of God."

May you, by reading and believing the Spirit-inspired Word of God, have the same saving faith in Jesus Christ!

BATTLE PLAN

Find a reading plan to help you read the entire Bible in one year. If you want an even greater challenge, also commit to memorizing one Scripture passage per month. Today's verse is a good place to start!

ABOUT THE AUTHOR

Joshua Cooley is the children's ministry director at Covenant Life Church in Gaithersburg, Maryland; a freelance writer; and a former full-time sports writer/editor with a journalism degree from Liberty University. His freelance work has been featured in a variety of publications, including *Sports Illustrated, Sports Spectrum, Fellowship of Christian Athletes* magazine, Focus on the Family's *Thriving Family* magazine, *Bethesda* magazine, the *Atlanta Journal-Constitution*, the *Baltimore Sun*, and the *Orlando Sentinel*. He has written for teenagers and children in *Highlights, Breakaway, Brio, Clubhouse,* and *Susie* magazines. Joshua also has cowritten two other books: *The One Year Sports Devotions for Kids* (with Tyndale House Publishers) and *Playing with Purpose: Inside the Lives and Faith of the Major Leagues' Top Players*. He lives with his wife and four daughters in Germantown, Maryland.